C# Evolution

Exploring the New Features from C# 7.0 - 13.0

Mike Gold

C# Evolution

Exploring the New Features from C# 7.0 - 13.0

Mike Gold

This is a Leanpub book. Leanpub empowers authors and publishers with the Lean Publishing process. Lean Publishing is the act of publishing an in-progress ebook using lightweight tools and many iterations to get reader feedback, pivot until you have the right book and build traction once you do.

© 2024 Mike Gold

Also By Mike Gold

Veil of Blood and Magic
Epic Python Coding: Interactive Coding Adventures for Kids
One of Me
Crafting Applications with ChatGPT API
Creating Video Games Using PyGame
Creating a Wordle Game in React and TypeScript

Contents

Chapter 1: Intro 1

Chapter 2: C# 7.0 - Refining Everyday Scenarios 5
    Out Variables and Their Impact on Code Readability ... 5
    Pattern Matching Enhancements, Including is and switch
        Statements 7
    Tuples and Deconstruction - Syntactical Sugar for Productivity 8
    Introduction of Tuples in C# 7.0 9
    Local Functions - Improving Encapsulation and Readability 12
    Ref Returns and Locals - Optimizing Performance for
        High-Demand Applications 13

Chapter 3: C# 7.1 Improvements 21
    Async Main Method - Simplifying Entry Points in Asynchronous Programming 21
    Default Literal Expressions - Reducing Boilerplate Code . 25
    Inferred Tuple Element Names - Enhancing Code Clarity 28

Chapter 4: C# 7.2 Improvements 33
    Span - Managing Memory More Efficiently 33
    Ref readonly Returns and In Parameters - Optimizing
        Performance 41
    in Parameters 43
    Private Protected Access Modifier - Fine-tuning Encapsulation 45

CONTENTS

Chapter 5: C# 7.3 Improvements **51**
Enhanced Pattern Matching Capabilities 51
Performance Improvements in Out Variables 54
Support for Fixed-size Buffers on Additional Types 55
Improved Overload Resolution 56
Reassigning Ref Local Variables 63

Chapter 6: C# 8.0 - Embracing Modern Programming Paradigms **71**
Nullable Reference Types - Addressing Nullability Issues 71
`#nullable enable` Directive 73
Asynchronous Streams with IAsyncEnumerable 78
Pattern Matching Enhancements: Switch Expressions, Property Patterns, Tuple Patterns, and Positional Patterns................................ 85
`using` Declarations - Managing Resources More Efficiently 98

Chapter 7: C# 9.0 - Simplification and Records **105**
Records - Immutable Reference Types for Value-based Equality 105
Init-only Properties - Making Object Initialization More Flexible.............................. 118
Top-level Statements - Simplifying Small Programs and Scripts 119
Pattern Matching Enhancements: Relational Patterns, Logical Patterns 124
Native Sized Integers for Performance-Critical Scenarios 125

Chapter 8: C# 10.0 - Further Refinements and Global Usings 131
Global Using Directives - Simplifying Project-wide Imports 131
File-Scoped Namespaces - Reducing Nesting and Improving Readability 131
Record Structs - Combining the Benefits of Records and Structs 132
Improved Lambda Expressions and Attributes on Lambda Expressions 137

    Constant Interpolated Strings - Enhancing Performance
        in String Manipulations 138

Chapter 9: C# 11.0 - Focused on Safety and Clarity 145
    List Patterns - Enhancing Pattern Matching with Collections 145
    Required Properties - Ensuring Object Initialization Integrity 149
    Raw String Literals - Simplifying the Representation of Strings 150
    Improved Definite Assignment - Reducing Nullability Warnings 155
    Async Method Builder Overriding - Customizing Task-Like Return Types 155

Chapter 10: C# 12.0 - The Latest Innovations 163
    Primary Constructors 163
    Collection Expressions 163
    Ref Readonly Parameters 166
    Default Lambda Parameters 166
    Alias Any Type 167
    Inline Arrays 167
    Experimental Attribute 168

Chapter 11: New Features in C# 13.0 171
    C# 13 Setup 171
    Params Collections: 172
    New Lock Type : 173
    New Escape Sequence: 176
    Method Group Natural Type Improvements: 177
    Implicit Indexer Access in Object Initializers: 182

Chapter 1: Intro

Welcome to an explorative journey through the recent evolution of C#, one of the most versatile and widely used programming languages in the modern development landscape. From its inception, C# has been at the forefront of innovation in the .NET ecosystem, continually adapting and growing to meet the challenges of software development. This book focuses on the transformative period from C# 7.0 to C# 12.0, a time during which the language has seen substantial enhancements that have significantly impacted how developers write code, manage data, and implement functionality in .NET applications.

The Purpose of This Book

The primary goal of this book is to provide a comprehensive overview of the changes and improvements in C# from versions 7 to 12.0. Each version brought specific features aimed at increasing the robustness, efficiency, and ease of coding in C#, making it a more powerful tool for developers. By understanding these changes, you can write cleaner, more efficient code, leverage the latest features to their full extent, and gain insights into the direction the language is heading.

What to Expect

We will embark on a version-by-version exploration, detailing the significant enhancements and the motivations behind them. Rather than just a listing of features, this book aims to delve into how these changes can be applied to improve everyday coding tasks, how they interrelate, and why they matter for modern software development.

- **C# 7.x Series**: This series of minor versions introduced

several features enhancing the functionality around data handling, performance, and code clarity. Notable introductions include tuples for grouping data, pattern matching for more expressive conditionals, and local functions to support encapsulation.
- **C# 8.0:** A major update focused on making C# safer and more robust, with the introduction of nullable reference types to tackle the nullability issues that have plagued developers for years. Asynchronous streams and enhanced pattern matching also highlight this version's push towards more modern, functional programming styles.
- **C# 9.0:** With this release, C# made significant strides in simplifying codebases with records and init-only properties, enhancing the language's capabilities to handle immutable data more naturally. Top-level statements and improved pattern matching were also introduced, streamlining the development of both large applications and small utilities.
- **C# 10.0:** Continued to refine the features introduced in earlier versions and added new ones such as global using directives, file-scoped namespaces, and record structs, all designed to reduce boilerplate and improve the readability and structure of code.
- **C# 11.0 and 12.0:** These versions focus on advancing language safety, clarity, and flexibility with features like list patterns, required properties, and enhancements to lambda expressions. Each addition is aimed at empowering developers to write more concise and reliable applications.

Structure of This Book

Each chapter of this book is dedicated to a specific version of C#, beginning with a detailed discussion of the features introduced in that version. Following the overview, we will delve into practical examples and scenarios where these features can be effectively utilized. This approach not only helps in understanding each feature's functionality but also provides insight into its practical application in real-world software development.

Prerequisites for Running the Examples

To fully benefit from the examples and exercises provided in this book, you will need to have a few tools and technologies set up on your system. The reader should have a working installation of **.NET 8.0 or later**, as it supports all the features of C# up to version 12.0. Additionally, an integrated development environment (IDE) such as **Visual Studio 2022** or **Visual Studio Code** with the C# extension installed is recommended for the best coding experience. Basic familiarity with C# and the general principles of programming will be very helpful, though the book will cover foundational concepts as needed. For each example, detailed instructions and code explanations will be provided to ensure that even readers with minimal prior experience in C# can follow along and understand the implementation details.

Who This Book Is For

This book is designed for a broad audience, ranging from novice programmers who have just started learning C# and want to catch up with the latest language features, to experienced developers looking to refine and update their knowledge of recent C# innovations. If you are a student of computer science looking to solidify your understanding of modern programming concepts, or a software professional aiming to enhance the quality and maintainability of your code, you will find this guide indispensable. We encourage hobbyists and tinkerers who enjoy exploring new programming paradigms and techniques to dive into this book as well. By presenting the material in a clear, engaging, and practical manner, this book aims not only to educate but also to inspire readers to leverage C# to its full potential in their personal and professional projects. No matter your background or level of expertise, this book will provide valuable insights and tools to help you excel in the evolving world of software development with C#.

As we proceed through this book, you'll gain a deeper understanding of how C# has evolved to meet the needs of modern developers and how you can utilize these advancements to enhance your development practices. Whether you are a seasoned C# developer or new to the language, this book will equip you with the knowledge to take full advantage of the capabilities of C# in your future projects. Let's begin this journey into the evolving world of C#.

Chapter 2: C# 7.0 - Refining Everyday Scenarios

The release of C# 7.0 marked a significant milestone in the evolution of the C# language, introducing several features aimed at refining everyday coding scenarios for developers. This chapter explores these features, explaining their purposes, and demonstrating their applications through examples.

Out Variables and Their Impact on Code Readability

Prior to C# 7.0, working with out parameters often required declaring variables far in advance of their actual usage, cluttering code and reducing readability.

You would need to declare the variable intended to hold the out parameter separately, before the method call. This meant more lines of code and sometimes less clarity, especially when the variable was only relevant within the scope of an if statement or similar construct.

Here's how you would typically handle the out parameter with int.TryParse before C# 7.0:

```
int result; // Variable declaration must
            // be done separately
if (int.TryParse("123", out result))
{
    Console.WriteLine(result); // Output: 123
}
```

In this example:

- The `result` variable is declared explicitly before the `int.TryParse` method call.
- The `out` keyword is used in the method call to indicate that `result` is an out parameter, which will be assigned within the method.

Key Differences and Implications

The requirement to declare `out` variables separately had a few implications:

- **Increased verbosity**: Additional lines of code were needed just to declare variables, which could clutter up methods, especially when multiple `out` parameters were involved.
- **Scope and lifecycle management**: Variables had to be managed over a broader scope than necessary. In C# 7.0 and later, `out` variables can be declared inline and scoped tightly within the `if` block or similar constructs, reducing their visibility and lifecycle management overhead.
- **Code readability and maintainability**: Early declarations required developers to track variables that might only be relevant in a specific conditional context. Inline declarations help keep the code concise and easier to read, as the declaration and usage are located in the same code block.

Transition to C# 7.0 and Beyond

The introduction of inline out variables in C# 7.0 was part of a broader effort to make the language more concise and to enhance its ability to handle common programming patterns more naturally. This change has been widely appreciated for making code cleaner and reducing the boilerplate often associated with rigorous type-safe coding practices in C#.

This feature, along with many others introduced in C# 7.0 and later versions, shows a clear intent to improve the developer experience by simplifying common tasks and enhancing language expressiveness.

C# 7.0 introduced inline out variables, allowing developers to declare variables at the point of their first use within method calls that have out parameters.

Example:

```
if (int.TryParse("123", out int result))
{
    Console.WriteLine(result); // Output: 123
}
```

Pattern Matching Enhancements, Including is and switch Statements

Pattern matching in C# 7.0 was enhanced with more expressive syntax, making it easier to work with types and conditions. The is keyword gained the ability to check a variable's type and assign it to a new variable if the check is successful. The switch statement was also enhanced to support pattern matching with cases that can match on type, value, or a combination of both.

Example:

```csharp
object obj = "Hello, World!";
if (obj is string s)
{
    Console.WriteLine(s.ToLower());
    // Output: hello, world!
}

switch (obj)
{
    case string str:
        Console.WriteLine(str.ToUpper());
        // Output: HELLO, WORLD!
        break;
}
```

In both the `if` statement and the `switch` statement, the code checks whether `obj` is of type `string` and simultaneously assigns the string to a variable for further use. This approach streamlines the process of type checking and variable assignment, allowing the variable to be immediately utilized within the respective blocks.

Tuples and Deconstruction - Syntactical Sugar for Productivity

C# 7.0 introduced tuples as lightweight data structures for grouping multiple elements. Tuples can be used to return multiple values from a method without defining a custom class or struct.

Before C# 7.0

Prior to C# 7.0, if developers wanted to return multiple values from a method, they typically used one of the following approaches:

1. **Out Parameters**: Using out parameters to return additional values. However, this method could be cumbersome and less clear, especially with multiple out parameters.

```
public void GetValues(out int x, out int y)
{
    x = 5;
    y = 10;
}
```

2. **Custom Classes or Structs**: Creating a custom class or struct to hold the multiple return values. This approach was more type-safe and clearer but required additional boilerplate code.

```
public class Coordinates
{
    public int X { get; set; }
    public int Y { get; set; }
}

public Coordinates GetCoordinates()
{
    return new Coordinates { X = 5, Y = 10 };
}
```

3. **Using Existing Tuple Classes**: .NET has always had Tuple classes in the System namespace, but these were not as syntactically convenient as the value tuples introduced in C# 7.0. These older tuples also didn't support deconstruction or have the performance benefits of the newer value tuples.

```
public Tuple<int, int> GetOldStyleTuple()
{
    return new Tuple<int, int>(5, 10);
}
```

Introduction of Tuples in C# 7.0

C# 7.0 introduced tuples in a more intrinsic and language-integrated way, using the `System.ValueTuple` type, which allows for lightweight tuple objects that can be deconstructed and support semantic names for the elements. This makes the code more readable and efficient.

```
public (int X, int Y) GetCoordinates()
{
    return (5, 10);
}

// Usage
var coords = GetCoordinates();
Console.WriteLine(coords.X); // Output: 5
```

These tuples can be returned from methods and deconstructed easily, which greatly simplifies scenarios where multiple related values need to be returned from methods without creating additional types.

Deconstructing Tuples

This code snippet illustrates the simplicity and power of using tuples in C# for returning multiple values from a method and deconstructing them for easy use.

```
(string, int) GetNameAndAge() => ("John Doe", 30);
var (name, age) = GetNameAndAge();
// Output: John Doe is 30 years old
Console.WriteLine($"{name} is {age} years old.");
```

Explaining the Code

1. **Function Definition with Tuple Return:**

```
(string, int) GetNameAndAge() => ("John Doe", 30);
```

Here, `GetNameAndAge` is a method that returns a tuple containing two elements: a `string` and an `int`. This method uses a tuple to return both a name and an age together without the need for a custom class or struct. The method leverages C#'s tuple syntax, where the types of the tuple's elements are defined in the method signature.

2. **Tuple Deconstruction:**

```
var (name, age) = GetNameAndAge();
```

This line demonstrates tuple deconstruction, where the returned tuple is immediately unpacked into two distinct variables: `name` and `age`. This process allows you to directly access each element of the tuple by a clear and meaningful variable name, enhancing the readability and usability of the data. The `var` keyword indicates that the variable types will be inferred by the compiler based on the tuple's structure, making the code cleaner and less verbose.

3. **Using Deconstructed Values:**

```
Console.WriteLine($"{name} is {age} years old.");
// Output: John Doe is 30 years old.
```

Finally, this line uses string interpolation to format and display the values retrieved from the tuple. The variables `name` and `age` are used directly in a `Console.WriteLine` statement, demonstrating how intuitive and straightforward it is to work with the data once it has been deconstructed.

Benefits of Using and Deconstructing Tuples

- **Simplicity**: Tuples allow for a straightforward way to package together a small group of values without creating a separate data structure.
- **Readability**: When tuples are deconstructed, each element can be assigned to a descriptive variable name, improving the clarity of the code that follows.
- **Reduced Boilerplate**: There is no need to define a class or struct just to return multiple values from a method, reducing the amount of boilerplate code and keeping the focus on the method's logic.

Caution on Using Tuples

While tuples are incredibly useful for certain cases, they should be used judiciously. If the tuple starts to incorporate more elements or the elements are not inherently related, or if you find yourself passing the same tuple structure across various parts of your application, it's likely a sign that a more formal structure, such as a class or struct, would be more appropriate. Such structures offer better encapsulation, can include behavior (methods), and improve the self-documenting nature of the code.

Local Functions - Improving Encapsulation and Readability

Local functions, functions declared within the body of another function, were introduced to improve encapsulation and readability. They can capture local variables of the enclosing method and are only visible within their enclosing context.

Example:

```
int Fibonacci(int n)
{
    int Fib(int value) => value <= 1 ?
            value : Fib(value - 1) + Fib(value - 2);
    return Fib(n);
}
Console.WriteLine(Fibonacci(5)); // Output: 5
```

The `Fib` function is declared inside the `Fibonacci` function, which restricts its scope exclusively to `Fibonacci`. This scoping is not just a limitation but a feature — it ensures that `Fib` is tightly encapsulated within `Fibonacci`, preventing external access to `Fib` and thus safeguarding it from being called where it's not intended to be used. This encapsulation enhances the reliability and maintainability of the code by ensuring that the internal computation details of the `Fibonacci` function are hidden from the outer scope.

Ref Returns and Locals - Optimizing Performance for High-Demand Applications

C# 7.0 introduced ref returns and locals, allowing methods to return a reference to a variable rather than a value copy. This feature is particularly useful in performance-critical applications where copying large structures is costly.

Example: The code example you provided showcases the practical use of `ref returns` in C#, but it can be expanded to more clearly illustrate why this feature can be particularly powerful, especially in scenarios involving large data structures or performance-critical applications.

Understanding Ref Returns

`ref returns` allow a method to return a reference to a variable, rather than a copy of the variable's value. This capability is particularly useful in the following contexts:

1. **Performance Optimization**: Avoiding the overhead of copying large structures. This is crucial in performance-critical applications where frequent access and updates to large data items occur.
2. **Direct Data Manipulation**: Providing the ability to directly modify elements in a data structure managed by a method, library, or API without exposing the structure itself or making a copy of the data.

Example: Managing a Large Matrix

Let's consider the following example involving a large matrix of data, where using `ref returns` can significantly enhance performance and memory efficiency.

```
public class Matrix
{
    private int[,] data;

    public Matrix(int size)
    {
        data = new int[size, size];
        // Initialize with some values, for demonstration
        for (int i = 0; i < size; i++)
            for (int j = 0; j < size; j++)
                data[i, j] = i + j;
    }

```

```
        // Method to find an element that matches a
        // certain condition
        public ref int FindElement(int target)
        {
            for (int i = 0; i < data.GetLength(0); i++)
            {
                for (int j = 0; j < data.GetLength(1); j++)
                {
                    if (data[i, j] == target)
                        return ref data[i, j];
                        // Return a reference to the matrix
                        //element
                }
            }
            throw new IndexOutOfRangeException(
                    "Element not found");
        }
}

// Usage
var matrix = new Matrix(10);
// Assume element '5' exists for simplicity
ref int found = ref matrix.FindElement(5);
found = 100; // Modify the element directly
             // in the matrix
Console.WriteLine(matrix.FindElement(100)); // Output: 100
```

Explanation of the Code

In this example:

- **Matrix Class**: Represents a large matrix of integers.
- **FindElement Method**: Searches for an element that meets a certain condition. When it finds the element, it returns a reference to the element in the matrix, not a copy. This means

modifications to the returned reference will directly affect the original matrix.
- **Performance Benefits**: If Matrix were very large, returning a copy of an element could be inefficient in terms of performance and memory usage. With `ref returns`, only the reference is returned, avoiding copying large amounts of data.
- **Direct Modification**: The example demonstrates modifying an element directly within the data structure. This is crucial for scenarios where immediate updates are needed on the data set without the overhead of additional method calls or data copying.

Conclusion

Using `ref returns` is particularly advantageous when you need efficient access and modifications to elements within a large or complex data structure without exposing the entire data structure or incurring the cost of copying data. It simplifies code management and enhances performance, which is critical in large-scale or high-performance applications.

Expression-bodied Members Expansion

C# 7.0 expanded the use of expression-bodied members to constructors, finalizers, and property accessors, enabling more concise definitions for these members.

Example:

```csharp
class Person
{
    private string name;
    // Expression-bodied constructor
    public Person(string name) => this.name = name;
    public string Name
    {
        get => name; // expression bodied getter
        set => name = value; // and setter
    }
}
```

Expression-bodied Finalizer Example

Using an expression-bodied member for a finalizer simplifies the syntax if the cleanup operation is straightforward and can be expressed in a single line of code. Here's how you can define an expression-bodied finalizer:

```csharp
public class ResourceHandler
{
    // Handle to an unmanaged resource
    private IntPtr nativeResource;

    public ResourceHandler(IntPtr resource)
    {
        nativeResource = resource;
    }

    // Expression-bodied finalizer
    ~ResourceHandler() =>
        ReleaseUnmanagedResources(nativeResource);

    private void ReleaseUnmanagedResources(IntPtr res)
    {
```

```
17          // Assume this method properly releases the
18          // unmanaged resource
19          Console.WriteLine(
20              "Unmanaged resources released.");
21      }
22  }
```

While expression-bodied members for finalizers offer a neat syntactical feature, their practical application should be considered carefully, prioritizing the IDisposable pattern for managing and releasing unmanaged resources. This approach not only gives better control over resource management but also improves application performance by reducing the impact on the garbage collector.

Throw Expressions - Simplifying Exception Handling

Throw expressions in C# 7.0 allow throw to be used as an expression, enabling it to be used in expression-bodied members, null-coalescing operations, and more.

Example:

```
1  public string Name { get; }
2  public Person(string name) => Name = name ??
3              throw new ArgumentNullException(nameof(name));
```

In the provided code, the constructor for the Person class initializes the Name property using the name parameter that is passed in. If name is null, it throws an argument exception with the name of the null property (in this case the property is **Name**) Here's how it works:

1. **Property Initialization:**

    - public string Name { get; } declares a read-only property called Name. Being read-only means that once Name is set (during construction), it cannot be changed afterward.

2. **Constructor Logic:**

    - `public Person(string name) => Name = name ?? throw new ArgumentNullException(nameof(name));` is the constructor for the `Person` class. This line uses the null-coalescing operator (`??`) to assign the `name` parameter to the `Name` property.
    - If `name` is not `null`, it directly assigns `name` to `Name`.
    - If `name` is `null`, it throws an `ArgumentNullException` to indicate that a `null` value for `name` is not acceptable. This is a safeguard to prevent the creation of a `Person` object without a valid name.

3. **Error Handling:**

    - The use of `throw new ArgumentNullException(nameof(name))` ensures that if an attempt is made to instantiate a `Person` object with a `null` name, the error is clearly reported. The `nameof(name)` part dynamically fetches the name of the parameter causing the issue, making the exception message more informative and useful for debugging.

This pattern enforces that every `Person` object is instantiated with a valid, non-null `name`, thereby maintaining data integrity and providing clear error messages for developers during debugging.

This chapter has explored how C# 7.0 has refined everyday scenarios for developers through the introduction of several features designed to improve code readability, performance, and productivity. By incorporating these features into their codebases, developers can write more concise, expressive, and efficient C# code.

Chapter 3: C# 7.1 Improvements

C# 7.1 introduced a handful of features aimed at simplifying code and enhancing readability and expressiveness. These incremental improvements have a significant impact on daily coding practices. Let's explore each feature, its purpose, and how it can be applied.

Async Main Method - Simplifying Entry Points in Asynchronous Programming

Traditionally, the entry point of a C# application, the `Main` method, did not support asynchronous operations directly. With the introduction of C# 7.1, the `Main` method can be defined as `async`, allowing asynchronous operations to be awaited directly within it. This feature simplifies the code structure for applications that perform asynchronous initialization tasks.

Example:

```
 1  class Program
 2  {
 3      static async Task Main(string[] args)
 4      {
 5          await DoSomeInitializationAsync();
 6          Console.WriteLine("Initialization Complete");
 7      }
 8
 9      static async Task DoSomeInitializationAsync()
10      {
11          // Simulate an asynchronous operation (e.g.,
12          // loading configuration)
13          await Task.Delay(1000);
14      }
15  }
```

The introduction of the `async Main` method in C# 7.1 and later versions opens up a variety of applications where asynchronous operations are crucial right from the start of the application. This enhancement is particularly useful in several types of applications:

1. Console Applications

- **Background Services**: Applications that perform background tasks, such as data processing or messaging services, can benefit significantly. They can initiate asynchronous operations, such as setting up connections or loading resources, directly in the `Main` method.
- **Utility Tools**: Tools that interact with APIs, perform I/O operations, or require any sort of asynchronous setup before performing their primary function.

2. Desktop Applications

- Although desktop applications (like those built with WPF or Windows Forms) typically have their own event-driven, asynchronous patterns facilitated by the UI thread, having an `async Main` can be useful for initializing resources before the main UI loads.

3. Web Applications

- While web applications typically rely on frameworks like ASP.NET Core that have their built-in mechanisms for handling asynchronous operations, standalone services or background tasks that support these web applications could use an `async Main` for initialization.

4. Microservices and Cloud-based Services

- Services that run in the cloud environment often require asynchronous operations at startup to establish database connections, configure services, or interact with other APIs. The `async Main` method allows these initializations to be handled efficiently.

5. Games and Real-time Applications

- Game development often involves loading assets or setting up game states asynchronously. Using an `async Main` allows for these operations to be streamlined into the application's entry point, improving the startup process.

6. API Clients and SDKs

- Applications designed to interact with APIs or utilize SDKs that perform asynchronous network calls can utilize `async Main` for setup and teardown operations, enhancing responsiveness and scalability.

Practical Examples of Using `async Main`

Here's how using an `async Main` could look in practical scenarios:

```
static async Task Main(string[] args)
{
    // Asynchronous network call to retrieve
    // configuration settings
    var config =
        await ConfigService.LoadConfigurationAsync();
    SomeService.Configure(config);

    // Asynchronous database connection initialization
    var database = await Database.InitializeAsync();
    Console.WriteLine("Database connection established");

    // Start the main part of the application
    StartApplication();
}
```

Advantages of `async Main`

- **Simplification**: Reduces the need for additional `async` wrappers or calling `.GetAwaiter().GetResult()` on tasks, which can lead to deadlocks if not handled carefully.
- **Readability and Maintainability**: Makes the code more linear and intuitive, especially for developers familiar with asynchronous programming.

Conclusion

The async Main method is versatile and can be used across different types of .NET applications, wherever asynchronous operations are required at the startup. It simplifies coding patterns, reduces boilerplate associated with asynchronous calls, and aligns well with modern programming practices that emphasize non-blocking, asynchronous operations.

Default Literal Expressions - Reducing Boilerplate Code

C# 7.1 introduced default literal expressions, which allow the use of default without specifying the type explicitly when the compiler can infer it. This reduces boilerplate code, especially when working with generics or initializing variables to their default values.

Example:

```
void SetToDefault<T>(ref T input)
{
    input = default;
}

int number = 5;
SetToDefault(ref number); // `number` is set to 0
Console.WriteLine(number); // Output: 0
```

Prior to C# 7.1, specifying the type with default(T) was necessary. Now, default alone suffices, making the code cleaner and more readable.

The default keyword in C# is used to obtain the default value for a given type. Before C# 7.1, you had to specify the type explicitly when using default, like default(int) or default(string).

However, with C# 7.1 and later, you can simply use `default` on its own, and the compiler will infer the type based on the context. This feature is particularly useful in reducing boilerplate code and making the code cleaner and easier to read.

How `default` Works

The `default` keyword returns the default value of a type. For:

- **Value types (like `int`, `bool`, `float`)**, `default` provides the "zero" value, which is 0, false, etc.
- **Reference types (like `string`, `object`, any class)**, `default` returns `null`.
- **Nullable value types (like `int?`)**, `default` returns `null`, as nullable types are treated like reference types in this context.

Examples of `default` Keyword Usage

Here are several examples showing how `default` can be used with different types of data:

1. With Value Types

```
int defaultInt = default;     // Equivalent to int
                              // defaultInt = 0;
double defaultDouble = default;  // Equivalent to double
                                 // defaultDouble = 0.0;
bool defaultBool = default;   // Equivalent to bool
                              // defaultBool = false;
```

2. With Reference Types

```
string defaultString = default;   // Equivalent to string
                                  // defaultString = null;
List<string> defaultList = default;   // Equivalent to
                                      //List<string>
                                      //defaultList = null;
```

3. With Nullable Types

```
int? defaultNullableInt = default;   // Equivalent to int?
                                     // defaultNullableInt = null;
```

4. In Generic Methods

default is particularly useful in generics where the type parameter can be any type, and writing specific code for each type category (value/reference) would be cumbersome:

```
public T CreateDefault<T>()
{
    return default;   // Correctly handles both value
                      // and reference types
}
```

In this generic method, default automatically adapts to the type T, providing either null or a zero-equivalent value depending on whether T is a reference or value type.

Why Use the default Literal

- **Clarity and Simplicity**: Reduces the amount of code necessary to initialize variables, especially in generic programming.

- **Type Safety**: Prevents type mismatches that could occur if initializing directly with literals like 0, false, or null. It ensures that the initialization is always appropriate to the type.
- **Maintainability**: Easier to maintain and update code, especially in generics or methods handling multiple types where the specific default values might not be directly evident.

Using the default keyword in these ways makes the code not only cleaner but also type-safe and easier to maintain, especially in complex applications involving generics and operations over multiple types. This feature is a clear example of how modern C# has evolved to make the code more intuitive and robust.

Inferred Tuple Element Names - Enhancing Code Clarity

With C# 7.1, when creating tuples, element names can be inferred from the variables used to initialize the tuple. This feature enhances code clarity by reducing redundancy and making tuple initialization more concise.

Example:

```
string firstName = "John";
string lastName = "Doe";
// Implicitly (string firstName, string lastName)
var person = (firstName, lastName);

Console.WriteLine(
    $"{person.firstName} {person.lastName}");
    // Output: John Doe
```

In the example above, the tuple element names `firstName` and `lastName` are inferred from the variable names used in the tuple's initialization. This automatic naming makes the code easier to understand at a glance and avoids the verbosity of explicitly naming tuple elements when it's clear from the context.

C# 7.0 introduced tuple types, which provide a way to group multiple values into a single compound value. From C# 7.1 onward, tuple element names can be automatically inferred from the names of the variables used in their initialization. This feature enhances readability and reduces verbosity in the code.

Here's a practical example that demonstrates this feature using a point coordinate system, where a tuple is used to represent a point with x and y coordinates:

Example: Inferring Tuple Names with Coordinates

Consider the following method that initializes and returns a tuple representing a point's x and y coordinates:

```
public (int x, int y) GetCoordinates()
{
    int x = 10;
    int y = 20;

    // Automatically infers the tuple names from the
    // variable names
    return (x, y);
}
```

Explanation:

- **Variables x and y** are initialized with values 10 and 20, respectively.

- When returning the tuple (x, y), C# automatically infers the names of the tuple elements based on the names of the variables used in the tuple's initialization. Thus, the tuple has named elements x and y.
- The return type of the method is defined as (int x, int y), but even if it were not explicitly defined with names, the names would still be inferred in the returned tuple.

Using the Tuple

Here's how you can use this method and access the tuple elements by their inferred names:

```
var point = GetCoordinates();
Console.WriteLine(
    $"Point coordinates: ({point.x}, {point.y})");
```

Output:

```
Point coordinates: (10, 20)
```

Advantages of Tuple Name Inference

- **Readability**: The code is easier to understand because the tuple's element names provide clear information about what data they hold.
- **Reduce Redundancy**: Avoids the need to explicitly specify names for tuple elements in the return statement, reducing redundancy and keeping the code concise.
- **Code Maintenance**: Enhances maintainability as changing the variable names automatically updates the corresponding tuple names without additional changes in the tuple creation syntax.

Conclusion

Tuple name inference in C# simplifies the handling of grouped data by reducing boilerplate code and enhancing the clarity of tuple operations. It's a small but powerful feature that leverages C#'s type inference capabilities to make tuple-related code more intuitive and less error-prone.

These improvements in C# 7.1, though seemingly small, contribute to cleaner, more expressive, and more efficient code. By embracing these features, developers can enjoy a streamlined coding experience, especially in scenarios involving asynchronous programming, initialization of variables to default values, and working with tuples.

Chapter 4: C# 7.2 Improvements

C# 7.2 continued the trend of refining the language with a focus on performance enhancements, memory management optimizations, and access control. This version introduced features that are especially relevant for high-performance applications and those that require fine-grained control over memory and access levels. Let's delve into these improvements, understanding their impact and how they can be applied through examples.

Span - Managing Memory More Efficiently

`Span<T>` and `Memory<T>` are two types introduced in C# 7.2 designed for memory management optimization. `Span<T>` provides a type-safe way to represent a contiguous region of arbitrary memory, while `Memory<T>` is similar but is designed to represent memory that might not be contiguous and is more suited for scenarios where a `Span<T>` needs to be stored for longer periods.

Span Example:

Chapter 4: C# 7.2 Improvements

```
void ProcessSpan(Span<int> numbers)
{
    // Example operation on Span
    for (int i = 0; i < numbers.Length; i++)
    {
        numbers[i] *= 2;
    }
}

int[] array = { 1, 2, 3, 4 };
ProcessSpan(array); // Passing an array as a Span
Console.WriteLine(string.Join(", ", array));
// Output: 2, 4, 6, 8
```

Memory Example:

```
async Task ProcessMemoryAsync(Memory<int> numbers)
{
    // Asynchronously process the numbers
    await Task.Delay(100); // Simulate async work

    // Use Memory<T> directly in async method
    var arraySegment = numbers.ToArray();
    for (int i = 0; i < arraySegment.Length; i++)
    {
        arraySegment[i] += 10;
    }

    // Copy the results back to the Memory
    arraySegment.CopyTo(numbers);
}

int[] array = { 1, 2, 3, 4 };
// Passing an array as Memory
await ProcessMemoryAsync(array);
```

```
20  Console.WriteLine(string.Join(", ", array));
21  // Output: 11, 12, 13, 14
```

Memory<T> and Span<T> are two types introduced in C# 7.2 that are pivotal for memory management optimizations in .NET applications. These types provide a way to work with contiguous regions of memory without copying their contents, which is crucial for performance in scenarios involving large amounts of data or high-performance requirements. Here's a deeper look at how these types are treated in memory and why you might want to use them.

Understanding Span<T> and Memory<T>

Span<T>

- **Stack-only**: Span<T> is a ref struct that can only be allocated on the stack, not on the heap. This restriction ensures that Span<T> instances are short-lived, which is ideal for temporary buffers or slices of arrays when you need to perform operations without allocating additional memory.
- **Slicing and Dicing**: Span<T> provides slice access to arrays, ArraySegment<T>, or pointers, allowing modification and access without creating new arrays.
- **Performance**: By avoiding heap allocations and not incurring garbage collection overhead, Span<T> is highly performant, particularly useful in high-throughput, low-latency scenarios such as parsers or processing buffers.

Memory<T>

- **Heap-friendly**: Unlike Span<T>, Memory<T> can be stored on the heap, making it suitable for use across async calls and storing larger chunks of data over time.

- **Convertible to Span<T>**: Memory<T> can be converted to Span<T> for synchronous processing and is thus as flexible while allowing for persistence and compatibility with asynchronous operations.

How They Are Treated in Memory

- **Span<T>**: Being a ref struct means that Span<T> instances are always stack-allocated, which avoids garbage collection overhead. The stack-only nature makes it exceptionally fast and suitable for high-performance scenarios but limits its use to synchronous methods and scopes.
- **Memory<T>**: As a regular struct, Memory<T> can be allocated on the heap. It holds onto a segment of memory, making it safe to use over async operations. It's treated more like a traditional object concerning memory allocation but without the overhead of copying data it references.

Why Use Span<T> and Memory<T> ?

1. **Efficiency in Data Processing**:

   - You might use Span<T> and Memory<T> when you need to manipulate slices of arrays or buffers without actually duplicating any data. This is particularly effective in scenarios like audio/video processing, real-time data feeds, or any server-side application that needs to manipulate large quantities of data quickly.

2. **Reducing Memory Usage and GC Pressure:**

- These types help minimize memory usage by avoiding unnecessary copies. For example, parsing strings or arrays can be done without creating substrings or subarrays. Less memory usage translates to reduced garbage collector (GC) pressure, which is critical in performance-sensitive applications.

3. **Interoperability**:

    - Span<T> and Memory<T> can interoperate seamlessly with arrays and pointers, providing a modern, safe alternative to pointer arithmetic commonly used in high-performance applications.

4. **Asynchronous Programming**:

    - Memory<T> shines in async scenarios where you need to retain access to a segment of memory across await boundaries, which isn't possible with Span<T> due to its stack-only nature.

Sample Use Case

Suppose you're building a web server that processes images uploaded in multiple formats. You could use Memory<T> to hold onto the image data while it's being converted and processed asynchronously and Span<T> to manipulate sections of this data synchronously for performance.

In the scenario where you are processing image data uploaded to a web server, you can utilize Memory<T> and Span<T> to manage and process this data efficiently. Here's a simplified example to illustrate how you might implement such a solution in a C# application, using hypothetical methods for image processing:

Example: Using Memory<T> and Span<T> for Image Processing

```csharp
using System;
using System.IO;
using System.Threading.Tasks;

public class ImageProcessor
{
    public async Task ProcessImageAsync(Stream
                                        imageDataStream)
    {
        // Step 1: Read the stream into a byte array
        byte[] imageData = await ReadStreamAsync
                                        (imageDataStream);

        // Step 2: Wrap the array in a Memory<byte>
        // for asynchronous processing
        Memory<byte> memoryImageData =
                    new Memory<byte>(imageData);

        // Step 3: Process the image data asynchronously
        await ConvertImageFormatAsync(memoryImageData);

        // Step 4: Further synchronous processing using
        // Span
        ApplyFilters(memoryImageData.Span);
    }

    private async Task<byte[]> ReadStreamAsync
                                        (Stream stream)
    {
        using (var memoryStream = new MemoryStream())
        {
            await stream.CopyToAsync(memoryStream);
```

```csharp
            return memoryStream.ToArray();
        }
    }

    private async Task ConvertImageFormatAsync(
                        Memory<byte> imageData)
    {
        // Simulate an asynchronous operation to
        // convert image formats
        await Task.Delay(500); // Simulating async work

        // Example:
        // Convert from one image format to another
        // This is where you'd use an image processing
        // library that supports asynchronous processing.
        Console.WriteLine("Image format converted.");
    }

    private void ApplyFilters(Span<byte> imageData)
    {
        // Simulate applying filters to the image data
        // Note: Span allows for modification of
        // the memory in-place
        if (imageData.Length > 0)
        {
            // Example of modifying the image data
            // directly
            imageData[0] = 0;
        }

        Console.WriteLine("Filters applied to image.");
    }
}
```

Code Explanation

1. **Read Stream into Byte Array**: The image data, typically coming from an upload stream, is first read into a byte array. This is a common practice as it allows for easier manipulation of the data in memory.
2. **Wrap in Memory<byte>**: The byte array is then wrapped in a Memory<byte> object. This allows the image data to be passed around and manipulated without additional copying, and it can also be safely used in asynchronous operations.
3. **Asynchronous Image Conversion**: The ConvertImageFormatAsync method simulates an asynchronous operation that might involve calling an external library to convert the image format (e.g., from JPEG to PNG). This is done asynchronously to not block the thread, which is crucial in a web server scenario.
4. **Apply Filters Using Span<byte>**: After the asynchronous operation, further image processing is done synchronously. Here, Memory<byte>.Span is used to obtain a Span<byte> from the Memory<byte> object. Span allows for direct, in-place manipulation of the memory. In this case, it simulates applying image filters by modifying the image data directly.

Benefits of Using Memory<T> and Span<T>

- **Efficiency**: By using Memory<T> and Span<T>, the code avoids unnecessary memory copies. Memory<T> can be used safely with asynchronous methods, and Span<T> is ideal for high-performance, in-place modifications on the same thread.
- **Clarity and Safety**: The code is more readable and safer compared to dealing with raw pointers or arrays directly, especially when passing data across asynchronous boundaries.
- **Performance**: Particularly in a web server environment, using these types minimizes memory usage and GC pressure,

which can significantly improve the throughput and responsiveness of the server.

This example illustrates a practical use of Memory<T> and Span<T> in a high-level application scenario, showing how they can be integrated into real-world applications for efficient and effective memory management.

Conclusion

In summary, Span<T> and Memory<T> are powerful tools for managing memory more effectively in .NET applications. They provide crucial performance benefits by allowing low-overhead manipulation of data buffers, are essential for high-performance applications, and help in writing cleaner, less error-prone code by abstracting complex pointer manipulations.

Ref readonly Returns and In Parameters - Optimizing Performance

C# 7.2 introduced ref readonly returns and in parameters, allowing methods to return references to variables (thus avoiding copying) while ensuring that the caller cannot modify those variables. This feature is particularly useful for high-performance applications that need to process large structures or data sets.

Example:

```csharp
public ref readonly int FindMax(in int[] numbers)
{
    int maxIndex = 0;
    for (int i = 1; i < numbers.Length; i++)
    {
        if (numbers[i] > numbers[maxIndex])
        {
            maxIndex = i;
        }
    }
    return ref numbers[maxIndex]; // Return a reference
                                  // to the max element
}

int[] array = { 1, 3, 5, 7, 6, 4, 2 };
ref readonly int max = ref FindMax(array);
Console.WriteLine(max);
// Output: 7
// max = 10; //This line would cause a compile-time error
```

The introduction of `ref readonly` returns and `in` parameters in C# 7.2 marked a significant enhancement for developers working on performance-sensitive applications, particularly those involving large data structures or complex object models. Let's dive deeper into these features to understand their importance and typical use cases.

`ref readonly` **Returns**

The `ref readonly` modifier allows a method to return a reference to a variable rather than a copy of the variable. This feature builds on the existing `ref` return feature, adding an important constraint: the caller cannot modify the returned variable.

Why Use `ref readonly`

- **Performance**: It reduces the overhead associated with copying large structs. By returning a reference, the system avoids the cost of copying an entire struct, which can be substantial for large structs.
- **Memory Efficiency**: Reduces memory usage by avoiding unnecessary data duplication.
- **Immutability Guarantee**: Ensures that although a reference is returned, it cannot be modified by the caller, maintaining the integrity of the data.

Example of `ref readonly`

Consider a scenario where you have a large read-only configuration object that you need to access frequently but never modify:

```
public class ConfigData
{
    private readonly LargeConfigStruct _config;

    public ref readonly LargeConfigStruct GetConfig() =>
                        ref _config;

    // Assuming LargeConfigStruct is a large struct
    public struct LargeConfigStruct
    {
        public int Data { get; }
        // Other large data elements
    }
}
```

In this example, `GetConfig` returns a `ref readonly` to a `LargeConfigStruct`. This allows efficient access to the large struct without copying it, while also ensuring it cannot be modified.

`in` Parameters

The `in` keyword is used to specify that an argument is passed by reference but should not be modified by the called method. This feature is analogous to `const` references in C++.

Why Use `in`

- **Performance**: Like `ref readonly`, `in` parameters allow the passing of large structs without the need to copy them, significantly improving method invocation efficiency when large value types are involved.
- **Safety**: Prevents the method from modifying the argument, ensuring data integrity especially when passing large data structures that should not be changed.

Example of `in` Parameters

Imagine a method that needs to process a large numeric data structure but should not alter the original data:

```
public class DataProcessor
{
    public void ProcessLargeData(in LargeData data)
    {
        // Process data without the ability to
        // modify the original data structure
        Console.WriteLine(data.Value);
    }
}

public struct LargeData
{
    public int Value { get; }
```

```
14        // Other large data elements
15    }
```

In this example, `ProcessLargeData` can access the `LargeData` struct efficiently without copying it and without any risk of modifying the original data.

Use Case Scenarios

- **High-Performance Computing**: Applications like scientific computing, financial models, or any system where performance and memory efficiency are critical.
- **Immutable Data Structures**: When working with data that must not change after creation, ensuring methods that read this data don't inadvertently modify it.
- **Game Development**: Games often involve complex data structures representing game state, player data, etc., which need to be accessed frequently and efficiently without modification during rendering or logic processing.

Conclusion

Both `ref readonly` returns and `in` parameters are crucial in scenarios where performance is critical, and data integrity must be maintained. They enable more efficient data access patterns while safeguarding the immutability of the data being operated upon, aligning well with modern practices that emphasize both performance and reliability in software development.

Private Protected Access Modifier - Fine-tuning Encapsulation

The `private protected` access modifier, introduced in C# 7.2, offers a new level of access control, allowing members to be accessible only within their declaring assembly and by derived classes. This modifier fine-tunes encapsulation by providing a more nuanced access level between `protected` and `private`.

Example:

```
public class BaseClass
{
    private protected int Value { get; set; }
}

public class DerivedClass : BaseClass
{
    public void SetValue(int value)
    {
        Value = value; // Accessible due to being a
                       // derived class
    }
}

public class AnotherClass
{
    public void AttemptAccess()
    {
        BaseClass baseClass = new BaseClass();
        // baseClass.Value = 10; // This line would
                                 // cause a compile-time error
    }
}
```

In this example, `Value` is accessible within `DerivedClass` because it is derived from `BaseClass`, but it is not accessible from `AnotherClass`, even though it might be in the same assembly.

The `private protected` provides an enhanced level of encapsulation beyond what the modifier `protected` provides. This modifier makes a member accessible only within its declaring assembly, as well as only by derived classes. This allows for fine-tuned control over data encapsulation and class design, particularly useful in scenarios involving complex inheritance hierarchies spread across different assemblies.

Example of `private protected` Restricting outside Assemblies

To demonstrate the usage of `private protected` and how it restricts access, let's consider two assemblies:

1. **AssemblyA**: Contains the base class with a `private protected` member.
2. **AssemblyB**: Attempts to access the `private protected` member from a derived class.

AssemblyA: Base Class Definition

First, let's define a class in **AssemblyA** that uses the `private protected` access modifier.

File: AssemblyA.cs

```csharp
// Assembly: AssemblyA
namespace AssemblyA
{
    public class BaseClass
    {
        private protected int ImportantData { get; set; }

        public BaseClass()
        {
            ImportantData = 42;
        }
    }
}
```

In this setup, `ImportantData` is marked as `private protected`, which means it can only be accessed within the AssemblyA and only by classes that derive from BaseClass.

AssemblyB: Derived Class Trying to Access `private protected`

Next, we'll create a derived class in a different assembly, **AssemblyB**, that attempts to access the `private protected` member from BaseClass.

File: AssemblyB.cs

```csharp
// Assembly: AssemblyB
using AssemblyA;

namespace AssemblyB
{
    public class DerivedClass : BaseClass
    {
        public void Display()
        {
            // This line will cause a compile-time error
```

```
11                Console.WriteLine(ImportantData);
12            }
13        }
14    }
```

Compilation Error

When you try to compile **AssemblyB**, you will encounter a compilation error:

```
1  error CS0122: 'BaseClass.ImportantData' is inaccessible
2  due to its protection level
```

This error occurs because `DerivedClass` in **AssemblyB** tries to access `ImportantData`, which is not accessible outside of its declaring assembly (`AssemblyA`), despite `DerivedClass` deriving from `BaseClass`.

Why Use `private protected`?

The `private protected` access modifier is particularly useful when you want to hide implementation details from external assemblies while still allowing extended functionality within an assembly. This is especially relevant in the development of libraries where control over class behavior and data is crucial, and you need to maintain a strict API boundary.

Summary

The `private protected` modifier allows developers to fine-tune access to class members, providing a way to secure data by limiting accessibility to the same assembly and derived classes only. This enhances encapsulation and protects against unintended usage or modification in complex software systems.

Chapter 4: C# 7.2 Improvements

C# 7.2's features are essential for developers working on high-performance applications, dealing with large data structures, or requiring precise control over access levels. By leveraging `Span<T>`, `Memory<T>`, `ref readonly`, `in` parameters, and the `private protected` access modifier, developers can write more efficient, safe, and encapsulated code.

Chapter 5: C# 7.3 Improvements

C# 7.3 further refined the language, focusing on enhancements that improve performance, make safe coding easier, and enable more flexible coding practices. This chapter delves into the notable features introduced in C# 7.3, providing detailed explanations and practical examples of each to help you incorporate these enhancements into your own projects.

Enhanced Pattern Matching Capabilities

C# 7.3 expanded on the pattern matching capabilities introduced in earlier versions, allowing for more complex and expressive conditions in `is` expressions and `switch` statements.

Example:

```csharp
object obj = 100;
if (obj is int i && i > 50) // Enhanced pattern matching
                            // with additional condition
{
    Console.WriteLine($"{i} is an integer and greater
                        than 50.");
}
// Output: 100 is an integer and greater than 50.
```

In C# 7.3, the improvements to pattern matching particularly extended to the use of `switch` statements, making them more versatile and powerful for handling multiple conditions and types. Let's look at an example where these enhancements are demonstrated using a `switch` statement with pattern matching on various types and conditions.

Example: Enhanced Pattern Matching in a Switch Statement with C# 7.3

This example demonstrates how to use pattern matching in `switch` statements to handle different types and conditions more effectively. The code checks various types of objects and performs operations based on their type and values:

```
public void ProcessObject(object obj)
{
    switch (obj)
    {
        case int i when i > 0:
            Console.WriteLine($"{i} is a positive
                                            integer.");
            break;
        case int i when i <= 0:
            Console.WriteLine($"{i} is a non-positive
                                            integer.");
            break;
        case string s when s.Length > 10:
            Console.WriteLine($"String is too long:
                    {s.Substring(0, 10)}...");
            break;
        case string s:
            Console.WriteLine($"String: {s}");
            break;
        case double d when d == 0.0:
            Console.WriteLine("Double is zero.");
```

```csharp
                break;
            case null:
                Console.WriteLine("Object is null.");
                break;
            default:
                Console.WriteLine("Unknown type or condition.
                                  ");
                break;
    }
}

// Demo calling the method
public void Demo()
{
    ProcessObject(15);   // Output: 15 is a positive
                         //  integer.
    ProcessObject(-1);   // Output: -1 is a non-positive
                         //  integer.
    ProcessObject("Hello");    // Output: String: Hello
    ProcessObject("Hello World from C# 7.3");
                         // Output:
                         // String is too long: Hello
                         //   Worl...
    ProcessObject(0.0);      // Output: Double is zero.
    ProcessObject(null);     // Output: Object is null.
    ProcessObject(new List<int>()); // Output: Unknown
                                    // type or condition.
}
```

Explanation

In the switch statement in the ProcessObject method:

- **Integer Matching**: It differentiates between positive and

non-positive integers. This is done using the `when` keyword, which adds a condition to the case label.
- **String Matching**: The code checks for string objects, further distinguishing them based on their length. Strings longer than 10 characters are trimmed and appended with ellipses.
- **Double Matching**: It checks specifically for a double that equals 0.0.
- **Null Checking**: There's a case for handling `null`, ensuring that the program can gracefully handle null values.
- **Default Case**: Handles any other types or conditions not specifically accounted for by the other case labels.

This example showcases the power and flexibility of pattern matching in `switch` statements in C# 7.3, enabling more clear and concise code when handling multiple types and conditions.

Performance Improvements in Out Variables

C# 7.3 introduced enhancements to `out` variables, particularly in the context of pattern matching, making the code not only more concise but also potentially improving performance by reducing unnecessary variable assignments.

Example:

```csharp
public bool TryParseDate(string dateString,
                         out DateTime dateTime)
{
    return DateTime.TryParse(dateString, out dateTime);
}

if (TryParseDate("2023-04-15", out var date))
{
    Console.WriteLine(
        $"Parsed date: {date.ToShortDateString()}");
}
// Output: Parsed date: 04/15/2023
```

Support for Fixed-size Buffers on Additional Types

Initially, fixed-size buffers could only be created with bool, byte, short, int, long, char, sbyte, ushort, uint, ulong, and float. C# 7.3 extended this support to additional built-in types like double and decimal.

Example:

```csharp
unsafe struct MyBuffer
{
    public fixed double Values[10];
}

unsafe void Demo()
{
    MyBuffer myBuffer;
    double* ptr = myBuffer.Values;
    for (int i = 0; i < 10; i++)
```

```
11      {
12          ptr[i] = i * 3.14159;
13      }
14  }
```

Improved Overload Resolution

C# 7.3 included improvements to overload resolution, addressing several situations where developers would previously encounter ambiguities. These enhancements help in selecting the most appropriate method overload more intuitively.

In C# 7.3, enhancements were made to overload resolution to address certain ambiguities that developers encountered in earlier versions. Overload resolution is the process by which the C# compiler determines which method overload to call when several methods could match the given arguments. This process relies on a number of rules regarding parameter types, number of parameters, and other factors.

Before C# 7.3, there were cases where the compiler could not clearly decide which overload was the best match, leading to either compiler errors or counterintuitive behavior. C# 7.3 introduced improvements that make overload resolution more predictable and logical, especially in complex scenarios involving generics, in modifiers, extension methods, and delegate conversions.

Example 1: Generic Constraints

Before C# 7.3, the compiler sometimes failed to select an overload based on generic constraints that made one of the overloads more specific than the others.

```csharp
public class Program
{
    static void Main(string[] args)
    {
        Test("hello");
    }

    static void Test<T>(T obj) where T : class
    {
        Console.WriteLine("Generic T where T : class");
    }

    static void Test(string text)
    {
        Console.WriteLine("Specific string");
    }
}
```

Before C# 7.3: The compiler might have chosen the generic method even when a more specific method (like the string overload) was available, leading to less efficient or unintended code execution paths.

With C# 7.3 and Later: The compiler correctly identifies and selects the more specific `Test(string text)` method as the best match when a string argument is provided.

Example 2: `in` Modifier

C# 7.2 introduced the `in` modifier for parameters, allowing them to be passed by reference but treated as read-only. However, overload resolution involving `in` parameters was not always intuitive.

```csharp
public class Program
{
    static void Main(string[] args)
    {
        int value = 10;
        Test(value);
    }

    static void Test(in int number)
    {
        Console.WriteLine("In int number");
    }

    static void Test(int number)
    {
        Console.WriteLine("Int number");
    }
}
```

Before C# 7.3: The compiler might have had difficulty deciding between the in modifier version and the normal version, especially if modifications or conversions were involved.

With C# 7.3 and Later: The compiler gives precedence to the method where the in modifier is not used if no modifications are necessary. This helps in scenarios where the in version could potentially restrict the usage of the variable inside the method.

Example 3: Better Handling of Nullable<T>

C# 7.3 also improved handling scenarios involving Nullable<T> types where method overloads could accept both T and T?.

```csharp
public class Program
{
    static void Main(string[] args)
    {
        int? value = 5;
        Test(value);
    }

    static void Test(int? number)
    {
        Console.WriteLine("Nullable int");
    }

    static void Test(int number)
    {
        Console.WriteLine("Int");
    }
}
```

Before C# 7.3: Ambiguities could arise when passing a Nullable<T> to overloads expecting either T or T?, particularly in cases where null values were involved or where implicit conversions were required.

With C# 7.3 and Later: The compiler more intuitively handles these scenarios, choosing the overload that best matches the Nullable<T> state (null or not null) and type, reducing unexpected behaviors.

Example 4: Better Handling of Tuple Literals

The improvements to tuple literal-based overload resolution in C# 7.3 focus on how the compiler chooses between method overloads when the arguments are tuple literals. This enhancement helps to resolve ambiguities more intuitively, particularly when method signatures differ only slightly in terms of tuple deconstruction.

Scenario Setup

Consider a situation where you have multiple method overloads that accept tuples, but the tuples might have different types. Here's an example that demonstrates tuple literal-based overload resolution:

Example Code

Let's define a class with multiple overload methods that take tuple arguments. Each method is differentiated based on the type of the tuple elements it expects.

```
using System;

public class TupleOverloadExample
{
    public void Process((int, int) point)
    {
        Console.WriteLine(
            $"int tuple: ({point.Item1}, {point.Item2})");
    }

    // Method with named tuple
    public void Process((double X, double Y) doublePoint)
    {
        Console.WriteLine(
            $"double tuple: ({doublePoint.X}, 
            {doublePoint.Y})");
    }

```

```
public void Process(double X)
{
    Console.WriteLine($"X: {X}");
}

public static void Main()
{
    var example = new TupleOverloadExample();

    // Tuple without element names
    example.Process((5, 10));

    // Tuple with element names call the same Process
    example.Process((X: 15, Y: 20));

    // Tuple with doubles call a different Process
    example.Process((X: 15.0d, Y: 20.0d));
}
}
```

Code Explanation

- **Two Overloads of `Process`:**

    - The first overload, `Process((int, int) coordinates)`, expects a tuple with two integer elements.
    - The second overload, `Process((double, double) coordinates)`, expects a tuple with two double elements.

- **Method Calls in `Main`:**

    - `example.Process((5, 10));` matches the first overload because the tuple provided consists of integers. This calls the version expecting a tuple with integer elements.

- `example.Process((5.0, 10.0));` matches the second overload because the tuple provided consists of doubles. This calls the version expecting a tuple with double elements.

C# 7.3 Improvement Impact

Before C# 7.3, the overload resolution process might not have effectively distinguished between these cases based solely on the tuple types when the types were ambiguous. With the improvements in C# 7.3, the compiler is better equipped to:

- Distinguish between method overloads based on the specific types of tuple elements provided in the call site.
- Select the most appropriate overload when multiple tuple types (e.g., integer and double) are available.

Practical Use

This feature is particularly useful in APIs or libraries where methods might need to differentiate based on the types of tuple elements. Having precise type-based overload resolution ensures that methods can implement different processing logic based on the tuple's element types, thereby improving code clarity and functionality.

Conclusion

The improvements in C# 7.3 help developers by reducing common ambiguities in overload resolution, making method dispatch more intuitive and reliable, particularly in complex scenarios involving generics, the `in` modifier, `Nullable<T>` types, and tuples. These enhancements contribute significantly to the robustness and maintainability of C# code, allowing developers to write clearer and more concise code without worrying about subtle bugs due to overload resolution issues.

Reassigning Ref Local Variables

With C# 7.3, developers gained the ability to reassign ref local variables. This improvement adds flexibility in scenarios involving references to different storage locations over the same scope. This approach is particularly useful when working with large data structures where performance is a concern since it avoids unnecessary copying of data.

The C# ref local and ref return features introduced significant enhancements to how references to variables can be handled within methods. These features allow methods to return references to variables instead of values, and allow the calling code to store these references in local variables. This approach is particularly useful when working with large data structures where performance is a concern since it avoids unnecessary copying of data.

Understanding ref Return and ref Local Variables

The Find method below demonstrates the use of ref returns, and how this returned reference is then stored in a ref local variable:

```
public ref int Find(int[] numbers, int target)
{
    for (int i = 0; i < numbers.Length; i++)
    {
        if (numbers[i] == target)
            return ref numbers[i];    // returns a
                                      // reference to the
                                      // array element
    }
    throw new IndexOutOfRangeException(
        $"{target} not found");
}
```

Detailed Explanation

The Find Method

- **Purpose**: Searches an array for a specified target value and returns a reference to the array element containing that value.
- **ref Return**: By using ref return, the method returns a reference to an element within the numbers array. This means that the method does not return the value of the array element, but a reference to the location of the element itself in the memory.

Usage of the Find Method

```
int[] array = { 1, 2, 3, 4, 5 };
ref int found = ref Find(array, 3);
Console.WriteLine(found);    // Output: 3
found = ref Find(array, 4);  // Reassign ref local to
                             // point to another element
Console.WriteLine(found);    // Output: 4
```

- **Ref Local Variable**: The variable found is declared as ref int. This declaration means that found does not just hold an integer value, but a reference to an integer. This allows found to directly refer to elements inside the array.
- **Assigning found**: Initially, found is set to refer to the array element that contains the value 3. When printed, it outputs 3.
- **Reassigning found**: The reference stored in found is then changed to refer to the array element containing the value 4. The subsequent print statement thus outputs 4.

Why Use ref Local Variables and ref Returns

- **Performance**: This feature is particularly useful when the values being handled are large structs, as it avoids the performance cost associated with copying large structs.
- **Mutability**: Changes made through the ref local variable directly affect the data in the original location, such as elements in an array. This allows for efficient in-place updates.
- **Safety and Control**: Unlike pointers in lower-level languages like C, ref returns and ref locals are type-safe, offering controlled mutability without the risk of pointer arithmetic.

To illustrate the benefits of using ref returns and ref local variables with large structures in memory more effectively, we can create an example with a more sizable and complex data type, such as a large structure representing a geometric shape or a data record. This will demonstrate the efficiency gains in terms of performance when avoiding the copying of large structures.

Example: Managing a Large Struct with `ref` Returns

Let's define a `LargeStruct` that simulates a substantial data structure, and create a method that modifies this structure directly using `ref` returns.

Define the Large Struct

First, we define a struct with multiple fields to simulate substantial memory usage:

```
public struct LargeStruct
{
    public int Id;
    public double Width, Height, Depth;
    public decimal Cost;
    public DateTime LastUpdated;
    public string TonsOfData

    // Constructor to initialize the struct conveniently
    public LargeStruct(int id, double width,
    double height, double depth, decimal cost,
    string tonsOfData)
    {
        Id = id;
        Width = width;
        Height = height;
        Depth = depth;
        Cost = cost;
```

```
            LastUpdated = DateTime.Now;
            TonsOfData = tonsOfData;
        }

        public void UpdateDimensions(double width,
            double height, double depth, string tonsOfData)
        {
            Width = width;
            Height = height;
            Depth = depth;
            LastUpdated = DateTime.Now;
            TonsOfData = tonsOfData;
        }
    }
```

Create a Class to Manage Instances of LargeStruct

Next, we create a class that contains a collection of these structures and includes methods to access and modify them:

```
public class Inventory
{
    private List<LargeStruct> items
                = new List<LargeStruct>();

    public Inventory()
    {
        // Initialize with some dummy data
      List<LargeStruct> list = new List<LargeStruct>();
      string myVeryLargeString = "MASSIVE STRING";
        // Initialize with some dummy data
        list.Add(new LargeStruct(1, 10.0, 20.0, 30.0,
                        1000m, myVeryLargeString));
        string myOtherVeryLargeString =
                        "OTHER MASSIVE STRING";
```

```
            list.Add(new LargeStruct(2, 15.0, 25.0, 35.0,
                        1500m, myOtherVeryLargeString));

            // refs can only point to items in arrays,
            // so we need to convert the list to an array
            items = list.ToArray();
        }

        // Method to find an item and return a ref to it
        public ref LargeStruct FindItem(int id)
        {
            for (int i = 0; i < items.Count; i++)
            {
                if (items[i].Id == id)
                    return ref items[i]; // Return a
                                         // reference to the
                                         // struct in the list
            }
            throw new Exception("Item not found");
        }
}
```

Demonstrate Using the `ref` Return

Finally, let's use the `Inventory` class and modify a `LargeStruct` without copying it:

```
 1  public class Program
 2  {
 3      public static void Main()
 4      {
 5          var inventory = new Inventory();
 6          ref LargeStruct item = ref inventory.FindItem(1);
 7          Console.WriteLine($"Original dimensions:
 8              {item.Width} x {item.Height} x {item.Depth}");
 9
10          // Update dimensions directly via ref local
11          item.UpdateDimensions(12.0, 22.0, 32.0,
12              "<hugeString>");
13          Console.WriteLine (
14              $"Updated dimensions: {item.Width}
15              x {item.Height} x {item.Depth}
16              ");
17      }
18  }
```

Output

This program demonstrates efficient manipulation of large structures. By using `ref` returns, it modifies the dimensions of a `LargeStruct` directly within the list without copying the entire structure. This results in significant performance benefits, especially noticeable when the structures are large or when such operations are frequent.

Conclusion

Using `ref` returns and `ref` local variables in C# provides a way to handle data more efficiently, reducing memory usage and improving performance by avoiding unnecessary copying. These features are especially valuable in scenarios where large data structures need frequent updates or when performance optimization is critical. They represent a powerful tool in the C# developer's toolkit, combining the efficiency of direct memory access with the safety and readability of high-level code.

C# 7.3 provided developers with tools to write more expressive, performant, and flexible code. Through its enhancements to pattern matching, overload resolution, and the expansion of fixed-size buffers, this version not only streamlined existing coding practices but also opened up new possibilities for performance optimization and code clarity. By integrating these features, developers can better manage complexity and enhance the efficiency of their applications.

Chapter 6: C# 8.0 - Embracing Modern Programming Paradigms

C# 8.0 introduced several key features that mark significant advancements in how developers can write safe, clean, and efficient code. This chapter explores these new features, providing a comprehensive guide to each and demonstrating their practical applications with examples.

Nullable Reference Types - Addressing Nullability Issues

Nullable reference types feature in C# 8.0 is aimed at making the handling of nulls explicit, and reducing the common issue of `NullReferenceExceptions`, which are often a source of bugs in .NET applications.

Let's take a look at the Person class below. It contains a property `Name` of type `string` and a nullable property `Middle` of type `string?`.

Example:

```csharp
#nullable enable
public class Person
{
    public string Name { get; set; } // Non-nullable
                                     // reference type
    public string? MiddleName { get; set; } // Nullable
                                            // reference type

    public Person(string name, string? middleName = null)
    {
        Name = name ?? throw new ArgumentNullException(
                                        nameof(name));
        MiddleName = middleName; // Allowed to be null
    }
}

static void DisplayPerson(Person person)
{
    Console.WriteLine($"Name: {person.Name}");
    Console.WriteLine($"Middle Name:
       {person.MiddleName ?? "Not provided"}");
}

var person = new Person("John");
DisplayPerson(person);   // Middle name outputs
                         // "Not provided"
```

When calling the DisplayPerson function, we know that MiddleName of type string? can be null since it is explicitly allowed to be nullable. Therefore, we must handle the case where MiddleName is assigned null. On the other hand, Name, which is of type string, can never be assigned null. Prior to C# 8.0, any string type could be null, and this was accepted by the compiler.

The introduction of nullable reference types is a significant feature that helps developers prevent null reference exceptions, which are a common source of bugs in many applications. The #nullable enable directive is crucial in this feature, as it allows you to explicitly declare whether reference types should be nullable or non-nullable. Here's a breakdown of how this works and what it implies in your code.

#nullable enable Directive

- **Purpose**: The #nullable enable directive enables nullable reference type annotations for a given block of code. It affects how the C# compiler interprets the code that follows: reference types declared without a ? are considered non-nullable, and attempting to assign null to these types will result in a compile-time warning (or error, depending on project settings).
- **Scope**: This directive only affects the code that follows it up to the next #nullable directive or the end of the file. You can disable the nullable context by using #nullable disable.

Code Explanation

```
#nullable enable
public class Person
{
    public string Name { get; set; } // Non-nullable
                                     // reference type
    public string? MiddleName { get; set; } // Nullable
                                            // reference
                                            // type

    public Person(string name, string? middleName = null)
    {
```

```
12          Name = name ??
13              throw new ArgumentNullException(nameof(name));
14          MiddleName = middleName; // Allowed to be null
15      }
16  }
```

Non-Nullable Reference Type: Name

- **Declaration**: `public string Name { get; set; }`

    - With `#nullable enable`, this property is declared as a non-nullable reference type. The compiler will enforce that Name cannot be assigned `null` without raising a compile-time warning.
    - Attempting to do something like `person.Name = null;` outside of a constructor or initializer where checks are bypassed will result in a compiler warning.

Nullable Reference Type: MiddleName

- **Declaration**: `public string? MiddleName { get; set; }`

    - This property is explicitly marked as nullable with the `?` suffix, indicating that it can hold either a `string` value or `null`. This distinction helps in code correctness checks and makes the codebase more predictable.

- The `#nullable enable` directive can be placed at different levels depending on the scope you want it to affect:

The `#nullable enable` directive can be placed at different levels depending on the scope you want it to affect:

Class Level

If you want to enable nullable reference types for a specific class or file, you can place the `#nullable enable` directive at the top of the file or before the class definition.

```
#nullable enable

public class Person
{
    public string Name { get; set; }  // Non-nullable
                                      // reference type
    public string? MiddleName { get; set; }  // Nullable
                                             // reference type
}
```

Project Level

To enable nullable reference types for an entire project, you can configure it in your project file (`.csproj`). Add the following property inside a `<PropertyGroup>`:

```
<Project Sdk="Microsoft.NET.Sdk">
  <PropertyGroup>
    <Nullable>enable</Nullable>
  </PropertyGroup>
</Project>
```

Solution Level

If you want to enable nullable reference types for all projects within a solution, you will need to configure each project's `.csproj` file as described above, as there isn't a direct way to enable it globally at the solution level. However, you can automate this process by using a common `Directory.Build.props` file, which applies the settings to all projects within a directory tree.

Create a `Directory.Build.props` file in the root directory of your solution with the following content:

```
1  <Project>
2    <PropertyGroup>
3      <Nullable>enable</Nullable>
4    </PropertyGroup>
5  </Project>
```

Summary

- **Class/File Level**: Place `#nullable enable` at the top of the file or before the class definition.
- **Project Level**: Add `<Nullable>enable</Nullable>` in the project file (`.csproj`).
- **Solution Level**: Use a `Directory.Build.props` file in the root directory of your solution to apply the setting to all projects within the directory tree.

Choose the scope that best fits your needs for enabling nullable reference types in your codebase.

Constructor and Parameter Checks

- **Constructor**: `public Person(string name, string? middleName = null)`
    - name: The constructor throws an `ArgumentNullException` if `name` is `null`. This is a runtime check ensuring that the non-nullable `Name` property is indeed not null when initialized.

– `middleName`: This parameter is optional and defaults to `null`. It is explicitly marked as nullable, reflecting that it's entirely valid for `MiddleName` to be `null`.

Implications of Assigning `null` to `Name`

If you try to assign `null` to `Name`:

- **Within the Constructor**: If you attempt to set `Name` to `null` directly in the constructor without the null-coalesce check (`name ?? throw`), or if the `name` argument itself is `null`, the `ArgumentNullException` will be thrown, adhering to the logic you've coded.
- **Outside the Constructor**: If you attempt to assign `null` to `Name` after the object has been constructed, with `#nullable enable`, the C# compiler will issue a warning indicating you are trying to assign `null` to a non-nullable reference type. This helps in catching potential null reference errors early in the development process.

Treating nullable Warnings as Errors

If you want to ensure that assigning null to a non-nullable string is treated as an error at compile time rather than just a warning, you can add the following to your project file:

```xml
<Project Sdk="Microsoft.NET.Sdk">
  <PropertyGroup>
    <Nullable>enable</Nullable>
    <WarningsAsErrors>nullable</WarningsAsErrors>
  </PropertyGroup>
</Project>
```

Conclusion

The #nullable enable directive in C# 8.0 and later is a powerful tool for making your code safer and more robust. It enables explicit handling of nullability in reference types, reducing the chances of runtime null reference exceptions and improving the overall reliability of your applications. By distinguishing between nullable and non-nullable reference types, it brings additional type safety and clarity to C# development.

Asynchronous Streams with IAsyncEnumerable

With C# 8.0, asynchronous streams were introduced via the IAsyncEnumerable<T> interface, allowing developers to implement asynchronous iteration over sequences that include awaitable operations, such as streaming data from a web service. Here is a basic code example that illustrates streaming data from a long running process to the console.

Example:

```csharp
public async IAsyncEnumerable<int> GetNumbersAsync()
{
    for (int i = 0; i < 5; i++)
    {
        await Task.Delay(1000); // Simulate async work
        yield return i;
    }
}

public async Task DisplayAsyncNumbers()
{
    await foreach (var number in GetNumbersAsync())
    {
        Console.WriteLine(number);
    }
}

await DisplayAsyncNumbers();
```

To provide a more complex and real-world example using IAsyncEnumerable<T>, let's consider a scenario where you need to stream market data for financial instruments. The data might be fetched from a remote API that pushes updates periodically (e.g., stock prices, forex rates). In this scenario, IAsyncEnumerable<T> is particularly useful because it allows handling each piece of data as soon as it arrives, asynchronously, without blocking the thread while waiting for the next data point.

Example: Streaming Market Data Using IAsyncEnumerable<T>

Let's define a MarketData class and simulate streaming this data asynchronously. The example will fetch market data updates, such as price changes, from a hypothetical data source.

Define the `MarketData` Class

```
public class MarketData
{
    public string Symbol { get; set; }
    public decimal Price { get; set; }
    public DateTime Timestamp { get; set; }

    public MarketData(string symbol, decimal price)
    {
        Symbol = symbol;
        Price = price;
        Timestamp = DateTime.Now;
    }
}
```

Implementing Asynchronous Data Streaming

```
public class MarketDataService
{
    private readonly Random _random = new Random();

    public async IAsyncEnumerable<MarketData>
                StreamMarketDataAsync(string symbol)
    {
        // Simulating a stream of market data for
        // a given symbol
        while (true)
        {
            // Simulate variable update intervals
            await Task.Delay(_random.Next(500, 2000));

            // Simulate a price change
            decimal priceChange =
                (decimal)(_random.NextDouble() * 2
```

```
                    - 1); // Random fluctuation between -1
                            // and +1

                    // Assume the base price is 100
                    decimal newPrice = 100 + priceChange;

                    yield return new MarketData(symbol, newPrice);
                }
            }
        }
```

Consuming the Market Data Stream

```
public class MarketDataConsumer
{
    public async Task DisplayMarketDataAsync()
    {
        var marketDataService = new MarketDataService();
        string symbol = "AAPL";

        await foreach (var data in
            marketDataService.StreamMarketDataAsync
                                            (symbol))
        {
            Console.WriteLine(
                $"Symbol: {data.Symbol}, Price:
                {data.Price}, Time: {data.Timestamp}");
        }
    }
}
```

Main Entry Point to Run the Example

```
public static async Task Main(string[] args)
{
    var consumer = new MarketDataConsumer();
    await consumer.DisplayMarketDataAsync();
}
```

Explanation

- **MarketData Class:** This class represents a single unit of market data, including the financial instrument's symbol, its current price, and a timestamp.
- **MarketDataService Class:** This class simulates fetching market data. The method `StreamMarketDataAsync` continuously generates new `MarketData` instances with simulated price changes and yields them asynchronously.
- **MarketDataConsumer Class:** This class is responsible for consuming the streamed market data. It uses an asynchronous foreach loop (`await foreach`) to process each piece of data as soon as it is available.
- **Use of `IAsyncEnumerable<T>`:** This interface is ideal for scenarios like streaming where the data is produced or fetched incrementally and consumers handle data in a non-blocking fashion as it arrives.

Conclusion

Using `IAsyncEnumerable<T>` for streaming market data, or similar scenarios, provides a powerful pattern for handling real-time data feeds in an efficient and responsive manner. It enables applications to be more scalable and reactive, which is essential in fields like finance where data rate and volume can be high, and timeliness is critical.

Default Interface Methods - Evolving Interfaces

C# 8.0 allows developers to define implementation methods in interfaces, not just their signatures. This helps evolve interfaces without breaking existing implementations.

Example:

```csharp
public interface ILogger
{
   void Log(string message);
   void LogWarning(string message) => Log(
               $"Warning: {message}"); //default
                                       //implementation


}

public class ConsoleLogger : ILogger
{
    public void Log(string message)
    {
        Console.WriteLine(message);
    }
}

ILogger logger = new ConsoleLogger();
logger.LogWarning("Low disk space");
```

In this example, the ILogger interface provides a default implementation for the LogWarning method, which simply adds a "Warning" label to any given message. Because LogWarning has a default implementation in ILogger, you are not required to implement LogWarning in your concrete class like ConsoleLogger unless you need a specific behavior.

However, you do have the option to override this default implementation in your class. This flexibility allows you to either use the provided default behavior or customize `LogWarning` to meet your specific needs. This adaptability makes it easier to manage different requirements across various implementations.

Having said that, there are certain considerations and potential pitfalls when using default interface methods in C#. While default interface methods provide flexibility and can help avoid breaking changes when evolving interfaces, they also introduce some risks and challenges. Here are the pros and cons of using a default interface method:

Pros:

1. **Backward Compatibility**: Default implementations allow interface evolution without breaking existing implementations.
2. **Reduced Boilerplate**: They can reduce code duplication by providing common functionality directly in the interface.

Cons:

1. **Maintenance Complexity**: Changes to default implementations can have widespread, unintended effects, as all implementing classes will inherit these changes automatically.
2. **Hidden Behavior**: It can be less clear where the behavior is coming from, especially for developers who are new to the codebase or not aware of the default implementation.
3. **Versioning Issues**: When dealing with library updates, changes in default methods might introduce subtle bugs if the implementing classes rely on the old behavior.
4. **Interface Purity**: Traditionally, interfaces define contracts without implementation. Adding behavior to interfaces blurs the line between interfaces and abstract classes.

Best Practices:

- **Use Sparingly**: Default interface methods should be used judiciously and primarily for backward compatibility.
- **Clear Documentation**: Ensure that default implementations are well-documented to avoid confusion.
- **Review Impacts**: Carefully review and test any changes to default methods to understand their impact on existing code.
- **Consider Alternatives**: Sometimes, an abstract base class might be a better choice if the shared behavior is complex or critical.

Example Scenario:

In your case, using a default implementation for logging warnings in the `ILogger` interface is practical and avoids duplication in simple scenarios. However, if the logging behavior becomes more complex or needs to vary significantly between implementations, it might be better to leave the interface method abstract and require explicit implementation in each class.

Conclusion:

While default interface methods are a powerful tool, they should be used with caution. It's important to weigh the benefits against the potential risks and complexities they introduce. Proper documentation, testing, and careful consideration of the use case can help mitigate these risks.

Pattern Matching Enhancements: Switch Expressions, Property Patterns, Tuple Patterns, and Positional Patterns

Pattern matching was significantly enhanced in C# 8.0, introducing more sophisticated ways to inspect and decompose data in a declarative style. These improvements allow for more expressive, concise, and readable code. Here's a breakdown of the key enhancements to pattern matching introduced in C# 8.0:

1. Switch Expressions

Before C# 8.0, `switch` statements were more verbose and less flexible. C# 8.0 introduced switch expressions, a more concise syntax that functions as an expression rather than a statement. This means that switch expressions return a value and can be directly used in variable assignments, return statements, etc. They also enforce that all cases must be exhaustive (i.e., all possible values must be handled or explicitly ignored using a discard _).

Certainly! To illustrate the contrast between the traditional `switch` statements and the new `switch` expressions introduced in C# 8.0, I'll provide two examples that achieve the same outcome: one using the traditional `switch` statement and another using the modern `switch` expression. These examples will demonstrate how to determine the classification of an animal based on its species.

Traditional `switch` Statement (Before C# 8.0)

Before C# 8.0, using a `switch` statement to handle multiple conditions required more verbose syntax and typically involved multiple break statements. Here's how you might categorize animals using a traditional `switch` statement:

```csharp
public class AnimalClassifier
{
    public string ClassifyAnimal(string species)
    {
        string classification;
        switch (species)
        {
            case "dog":
                classification = "Mammal";
                break;
            case "crocodile":
                classification = "Reptile";
                break;
            case "robin":
                classification = "Bird";
                break;
            default:
                classification = "Unknown";
                break;
        }
        return classification;
    }
}
```

Switch Expression (Introduced in C# 8.0)

C# 8.0 introduced `switch` expressions, which are more concise and enforce exhaustive case handling. Here's how the same functionality can be implemented using a `switch` expression:

```csharp
public class AnimalClassifier
{
    public string ClassifyAnimal(string species) =>
        species switch
        {
            "dog" => "Mammal",
            "crocodile" => "Reptile",
            "robin" => "Bird",
            _ => "Unknown"   // Discard case handles all
                             // other possibilities
        };
}
```

Usage Example

Here's how you might use either version of the `AnimalClassifier` in a program:

```csharp
public static void Main(string[] args)
{
    var classifier = new AnimalClassifier();
    Console.WriteLine(
     classifier.ClassifyAnimal("dog"));
    // Outputs: Mammal
    Console.WriteLine(
        classifier.ClassifyAnimal("crocodile"));
        // Outputs: Reptile
    Console.WriteLine(
        classifier.ClassifyAnimal("robin"));
        // Outputs: Bird
    Console.WriteLine(
        classifier.ClassifyAnimal("shark"));
        // Outputs: Unknown
}
```

Key Differences and Advantages

- **Conciseness**: The `switch` expression is more concise and easier to read. It directly returns a value based on the matched case and eliminates the need for `break` statements.
- **Immutability and Purity**: `switch` expressions are expressions, not statements, which means they always return a value and can easily be used where immutability and functional programming patterns are preferred.
- **Exhaustiveness**: The use of the discard pattern _ in `switch` expressions ensures that all possible input values are accounted for, reducing the likelihood of unhandled cases.

These enhancements make `switch` expressions a powerful addition to C# for writing cleaner, safer, and more maintainable code, especially when dealing with multiple conditional logic paths.

2. Property Patterns

The provided code example effectively demonstrates the use of **property patterns** in C#, a feature that was significantly enhanced with the introduction of C# 8.0. Property patterns enable matching directly on the properties of an object within a switch case, which facilitates expressing complex conditional logic in a clear and concise manner.

Code Example: Using Property Patterns in C#

Here is a revised example that exclusively uses property patterns for demonstrating pattern matching in a switch expression:

```csharp
public class Person
{
    public string Name { get; set; }
    public string Location { get; set; }
    public int Age { get; set; }

    public string Greet() => this switch
    {
        { Location: "New York" } =>
                    $"Hello from New York.",
        { Location: "California" } =>
                    "Hello from California!",
        _ => "Greetings from somewhere on Earth!"
    };
}
```

Explanation of the Example:

- **Greet Method**: This method uses property patterns within a `switch` expression to generate greetings based on the person's `Location`. It matches the `Location` property of the `Person` object to provide a customized greeting:
    - `{ Location: "New York" }`: Matches a `Person` object where the `Location` is exactly "New York".
    - `{ Location: "California" }`: Matches a `Person` object where the `Location` is exactly "California".
    - `_`: The discard pattern acts as a default case for all other scenarios not covered by the specified patterns, greeting from "somewhere on Earth".

Breakdown of the Property Pattern

Property patterns allow the properties of an object to be directly matched within a switch case, making the code more readable and reducing the need for multiple if-else conditions or manual property checks. In the context of the Person class, this feature is crucial for evaluating conditions that depend solely on one property (Location) without considering other properties or values.

Why Use Property Patterns?

1. **Clarity and Readability**: Property patterns provide a direct and intuitive way to express conditions based on object properties, significantly reducing boilerplate code compared to traditional conditional checks (such as nested if-else statements).
2. **Enhanced Logic Expression**: They simplify the specification of complex conditions involving object properties in a single line of code, improving the overall organization and maintainability of the code.

Practical Implications

Property patterns are particularly useful in scenarios where the behavior of a method depends on the state of an object's properties. They are commonly used in routing decisions, UI logic, validation frameworks, and anywhere else complex conditions based on object properties are required.

This streamlined approach to handling properties within pattern matching not only enhances the power and flexibility of C# but also aligns it more closely with functional programming patterns where immutability and expression-based logic are prevalent.

3. Tuple Patterns

Tuple patterns allow for pattern matching against the elements of a tuple, combining the power of tuples with the expressiveness of pattern matching. This can be used in switch expressions to perform actions based on multiple values, simplifying complex conditional logic involving tuples.

Detailed Explanation of Tuple Patterns

Tuple patterns in C# enable pattern matching directly on the elements of a tuple. This feature significantly enhances the expressiveness and readability of code that needs to make decisions based on multiple values simultaneously. Using tuple patterns in switch expressions allows developers to deconstruct tuples within the switch cases and match each part of the tuple against specific conditions.

How Tuple Patterns Work

In a tuple pattern, you can match against the specific values of a tuple's elements. This approach is particularly useful when you want to execute different logic based on various combinations of tuple values. For example, you might use tuple patterns in scenarios where you need to check multiple values returned from a method and respond differently based on these values.

Example: Using Tuple Patterns in a Switch Expression

Let's consider a practical example where tuple patterns can be used effectively. Suppose you have a method that determines the operation mode and status of a device, both of which are returned as a tuple. You could use tuple patterns in a switch expression to handle various combinations of mode and status.

Scenario

Imagine you're developing a monitoring system for a network of sensors. Each sensor can operate in multiple modes (e.g., "Active",

"Standby", "Maintenance") and can report various status conditions (e.g., "OK", "Error", "Warning"). You need to perform different actions based on the combination of mode and status.

Code Implementation

```
public class SensorMonitor
{
    public enum Mode { Active, Standby, Maintenance }
    public enum Status { OK, Error, Warning }

    public (Mode, Status) GetSensorState()
    {
        // This method would realistically check the
        // sensor's state. Here, we just return a
        // simulated tuple for demonstration.
        return (Mode.Active, Status.Warning);
    }

    public void ProcessSensorState()
    {
        var state = GetSensorState();

        string action = state switch
        {
            (Mode.Active, Status.OK) =>
                        "Continue monitoring.",
            (Mode.Active, Status.Error) =>
                        "Initiate repair.",
            (Mode.Active, Status.Warning) =>
                        "Check sensor readings.",
            (Mode.Standby, Status.OK) =>
                        "Keep in standby.",
            (Mode.Standby, Status.Error) =>
                        "Alert maintenance team.",
            (Mode.Maintenance, _) =>
```

Chapter 6: C# 8.0 - Embracing Modern Programming Paradigms

```
31             "Maintenance mode - no action required.",
32             _ => "Unknown state."
33         };
34
35         Console.WriteLine($"Action: {action}");
36     }
37 }
```

Usage Example

```
1 public static void Main(string[] args)
2 {
3     var monitor = new SensorMonitor();
4     monitor.ProcessSensorState();  // Output depends on
5                                    // the simulated state
6                                    // returned by
7                                    // GetSensorState()
8 }
```

Key Points and Benefits

- **Simplification of Complex Logic**: Tuple patterns in switch expressions simplify handling multiple discrete conditions that depend on several variables. Instead of nested if-else structures, you can lay out all possible states and their corresponding actions in a clear and linear fashion.
- **Readability and Maintainability**: This approach improves readability and maintainability, as each case in the switch statement is easy to read and understand. Adding new cases or modifying existing ones becomes straightforward.
- **Exhaustive Handling**: Using _ for one or more elements in tuple patterns (as shown with (Mode.Maintenance, _)) allows for flexible matching, where certain elements of the tuple can be ignored if they are irrelevant for specific cases. This also

ensures that all possible combinations are considered, even if some are grouped together for a common action.

Overall, tuple patterns in C# provide a powerful tool for developers to handle multi-dimensional decision logic cleanly and efficiently, reducing errors and improving code quality.

4. Positional Patterns

Positional patterns work with types that have deconstructors. They allow matching based on the positionally deconstructed elements of an object. For instance, if a type deconstructs into three values, a positional pattern can match against these values in a single concise expression.

Understanding Positional Patterns

Positional patterns in C# leverage the deconstructor of a type to allow pattern matching against the components that a type can be broken down into. This method provides a concise and intuitive way to access data within complex types directly within a pattern-matching construct such as a `switch` expression or statement.

Deconstructors in C#

Before we delve into positional patterns, it's important to understand the concept of deconstructors in C#. A deconstructor is a method in a class or struct that enables the object to be "deconstructed" into its constituent parts. This method is usually defined using the `void Deconstruct(out ...)` syntax, where the method parameters define the parts into which the object should be deconstructed.

Example: Class with a Deconstructor

Consider a Person class where each instance has a Name and an Age. We can define a deconstructor for this class that allows it to be deconstructed into these two properties:

```
public class Person
{
    public string Name { get; set; }
    public int Age { get; set; }

    public Person(string name, int age)
    {
        Name = name;
        Age = age;
    }

    // Deconstructor
    public void Deconstruct(out string name, out int age)
    {
        name = this.Name;
        age = this.Age;
    }
}
```

Using Positional Patterns with the Person Class

With the Person class and its deconstructor in place, we can use positional patterns to match against individual Person instances based on their Name and Age:

```csharp
public void GreetPerson(Person person)
{
    var response = person switch
    {
        ("Alice", 30) =>
            "Hello Alice, who is 30 years old.",
        ("Bob", _) =>
            "Hello Bob, of undisclosed age.",
        var (name, age) =>
            $"Hello {name}, who is {age} years old."
    };

    Console.WriteLine(response);
}
```

Explanation of the Code

- **Pattern Matching in Switch Expression**: The `switch` expression uses positional patterns to match the properties of the `Person` object.

  - The case (`"Alice"`, 30) checks if the `Person`'s `Name` is "Alice" and `Age` is 30.
  - The case (`"Bob"`, _) checks if the `Name` is "Bob" and ignores the `Age`.
  - The `var` (name, age) case acts as a catch-all, capturing any `Person` and deconstructing it into `name` and `age`, which are then used in the response string.

Benefits of Using Positional Patterns

1. **Clarity**: The use of positional patterns allows the code to clearly and directly express the intent to match objects based on their decomposed properties.

2. **Simplicity**: Reduces the need for multiple `if-else` statements or manual checks against object properties.
3. **Flexibility**: Enables more complex matching scenarios that are readable and concise, especially useful in cases where multiple properties determine the execution flow.

Conclusion

Positional patterns provide a powerful way to deconstruct and match against the properties of objects in a single, concise expression. This feature is particularly useful in scenarios where objects are rich with data and decisions need to be made based on this data. It simplifies code and enhances its readability, making it easier to maintain and understand.

5. Using Declarations

While not a part of pattern matching, `using declarations` are another significant feature introduced in C# 8.0. They automatically dispose of objects at the end of the scope, simplifying resource management especially in conjunction with pattern matching when resources are involved.

Summary

C# 8.0 greatly enhanced pattern matching by introducing more powerful, flexible, and expressive features. These changes make C# a more functional language, especially beneficial for handling complex data manipulations and conditions cleanly and efficiently. Each addition helps developers write more declarative and less error-prone code, particularly useful in domains involving complex data processing, such as financial analysis, data science, or backend services handling varied data structures.

`using` Declarations - Managing Resources More Efficiently

The code snippet below demonstrates the use of the `using var` statement, a feature introduced in C# 8.0 that simplifies the management of resources that need to be disposed of after use. This particular syntax is an enhancement of the traditional `using` statement, providing a more concise way to handle resource cleanup automatically.

Example:

```
public static void ReadData(string filePath)
{
    using var file = new StreamReader(filePath);
    Console.WriteLine(file.ReadLine());
}
```

Explanation of the `using var` Statement

The Role of `using var`

- **Resource Management**: The `using var` statement ensures that the `StreamReader` object (`file`) is properly disposed of once it exits the scope where it was declared. This is crucial for types like `StreamReader` that access unmanaged resources, in this case, a file handle.
- **Automatic Disposal**: At the end of the method, when the `file` variable goes out of scope, the `Dispose()` method is automatically called on the `StreamReader` object. This method call releases the file handle and any other resources held by the `StreamReader`.

How `using var` Works

- **Simplified Syntax**: Unlike the older `using` statement, which requires braces {} to define the scope of the resource, `using var` does not necessarily need them. The scope of the resource disposal is tied to the scope of the variable itself, which in this case, is the method scope.
- **Scope and Disposal**: As soon as the execution exits the method in which `file` was declared, the `Dispose()` method of the `StreamReader` object is called. This automatic disposal happens regardless of how the method execution is terminated, whether it be a return statement or the end of the method block.

Benefits of `using var`

- **Cleaner Code**: This syntax reduces boilerplate code by eliminating the need for additional braces, making the code cleaner and easier to read.
- **Enhanced Safety**: It prevents resource leaks by ensuring that the resource is disposed of correctly, even if an exception is thrown within the block that might otherwise have prevented a manual call to `Dispose()`.
- **Local Scope Management**: By tying resource management to variable scope, `using var` clearly delineates resource lifetime, which can help reduce errors in resource management, especially in more complex methods.

In our specific example, `ReadData` reads the first line of a file specified by `filePath`. This operation can leave a file handle open if not properly managed, which can lead to file access issues in other parts of the application or other applications. The `using var` statement automatically takes care of closing the file handle:

```csharp
public static void ReadData(string filePath)
{
    using var file = new StreamReader(filePath);
    Console.WriteLine(file.ReadLine());
    // The file is automatically closed here,
    // even if an exception is thrown above.
}
```

Conclusion

The using var statement in C# 8.0 is a syntactic sugar that helps manage the lifecycle of disposable objects more conveniently and safely. It's particularly useful for dealing with I/O operations, database connections, or any other operations involving disposable resources, ensuring that resources are properly cleaned up without requiring extensive boilerplate code for exception-safe disposal.

Readonly Member Enhancements

```csharp
public class ImmutablePerson
{
    public string Name { get; }
    public readonly int Age;

    public ImmutablePerson(string name, int age)
    {
        Name = name;
        Age = age;
    }
}

var person = new ImmutablePerson("Jane", 30);
Console.WriteLine(
    $"Name: {person.Name}, Age: {person.Age}");
```

Static Local Functions and

Static local functions in C# 8.0 prevent capturing any variables from the enclosing method, offering a performance benefit by avoiding unintended allocations of closures.

Example: Static Multiply Method

Here's how you would define and use the `Multiply` method if it is standalone and static:

```csharp
public static int Multiply(int x)
{
    return MultiplyByFactor(x);

    static int MultiplyByFactor(int number) => number * 2;
}

// Usage
int result = Multiply(5);
Console.WriteLine(result); // Output: 10
```

In this setup:

- The `Multiply` method is a static method, meaning it can be called without creating an instance of a class.
- Inside `Multiply`, there is a static local function called `MultiplyByFactor`. This function is also static, scoped only within the `Multiply` method, and it does not capture any variables from the outer method, thereby improving performance and avoiding closures.

Explanation of Static Local Functions

Static local functions are defined within the body of another function. They can be useful when you want to prevent the local function from capturing any variables defined in its enclosing scope. This prevents potential errors and improves performance by avoiding heap allocation for closures.

Calling Multiply Method

You call the `Multiply` method directly since it's static. You don't need to instantiate a class or provide a class name (unless it is encapsulated within a class, which is not the case here as per your scenario). This makes the method easy to access and use wherever needed in your code, as long as it is accessible within the scope or namespace.

This direct approach is ideal in scenarios where you need a utility function that operates independently of any object's state, making the function more like a tool rather than a part of an object's behavior.

This chapter showcases how C# 8.0 supports modern programming paradigms that enable developers to write safer, more efficient, and cleaner code. Each new feature brought forward in this version addresses key aspects of software development, from handling nullability to enhancing interface design, thus providing powerful tools for developers in their everyday coding tasks.

Chapter 7: C# 9.0 - Simplification and Records

C# 9.0 brought significant simplifications and enhancements to the C# language, aiming to streamline coding patterns, improve performance, and provide new constructs for defining data-centric types. This chapter explores these new features, offering explanations and examples to help you understand and utilize them effectively.

Records - Immutable Reference Types for Value-based Equality

Records are a new feature in C# 9.0 designed to make it easier to create immutable reference types that behave more like value types. Records provide built-in functionality for value-based equality checks rather than the reference-based equality provided by traditional classes.

Example:

```
public record Person(string FirstName, string LastName);

var person1 = new Person("John", "Doe");
var person2 = new Person("John", "Doe");
Console.WriteLine(person1 == person2); // Output: True
```

Let's break down the code and explain more about records in C#:

Code Explanation

1. Record Declaration

```
public record Person(string FirstName, string LastName);
```

- **Record Type:** This line defines a record named `Person` with two properties: `FirstName` and `LastName`.
- **Positional Syntax:** The properties are defined using positional syntax within the parentheses. This is a concise way to define a record with properties.
- **Immutability and Value Equality:** By default, records are immutable and provide value-based equality. This means that two instances of a record are considered equal if all their properties have the same values.

2. Creating Instances of the Record

```
var person1 = new Person("John", "Doe");
var person2 = new Person("John", "Doe");
```

- **Instance Creation:** Here, two instances of the `Person` record are created. Both `person1` and `person2` are initialized with the same values for `FirstName` and `LastName`.

3. Comparing Instances

```
Console.WriteLine(person1 == person2); // Output: True
```

- **Equality Check:** The equality operator (==) is used to compare `person1` and `person2`.

- **Value Equality**: For records, the equality operator checks for value equality rather than reference equality. This means it compares the values of the properties of the records.
- **Output**: Since person1 and person2 have the same values for FirstName and LastName, the comparison person1 == person2 evaluates to True, and True is printed to the console.

Key Features of Records Demonstrated:

1. **Value-based Equality**:

    - Unlike classes, where the default equality comparison is reference-based (i.e., checking if both variables point to the same instance), records compare the values of their properties.
    - person1 and person2 are considered equal because their FirstName and LastName properties have the same values.

2. **Concise Syntax**:

    - The positional syntax for defining records allows for a concise and readable way to define immutable data models.
    - The declaration `public record Person(string FirstName, string LastName);` automatically creates properties, a constructor, and methods like Equals and GetHashCode at compile time.

3. **Immutability**:

    - Records are immutable by default, meaning the properties of a record cannot be changed after the record is created. This ensures that the state of a record instance remains constant.

Example of Creating a New Record with Modified Properties

If you want to create a new record based on an existing one but with some modified properties, you can use the `with` expression:

```
1  var person3 = person1 with { LastName = "Smith" };
2  Console.WriteLine(person3);
3  // Output: Person { FirstName = John, LastName = Smith }
```

- This demonstrates how you can create a new `Person` record instance (`person3`) with the same `FirstName` as `person1` but a different `LastName`.

Can a `record` have methods?

Yes, a `record` in C# can also have methods. Just like classes, records can contain instance methods, static methods, and can override methods such as `ToString`, `Equals`, and `GetHashCode`. Here's an example to illustrate how you can define and use methods within a record:

Example of a `record` with Methods

```csharp
public record Employee(string FirstName, string LastName)
{
    // Instance method
    public string FullName() => $"{FirstName} {LastName}";

    // Static method
    public static Employee CreateAnonymous()
    {
        return new Employee("John", "Doe");
    }

    // Override ToString method for custom string
    // representation
    public override string ToString()
    {
        return $"Employee: {FullName()}";
    }

    // Method to greet another person
    public string Greet(Employee other)
    {
        return $"Hello {other.FirstName}, I am
                            {FullName()}";
    }
}

public class Program
{
    public static void Main()
    {
        Employee employee1 = new Employee("Alice",
                                    "Johnson");
        Employee employee2 = new Employee("Bob", "Smith");

        // Using the FullName method
```

```
Console.WriteLine(employee1.FullName());

// Using the static CreateAnonymous method
Employee anonymous = Employee.CreateAnonymous();
Console.WriteLine(anonymous);

// Using the Greet method
Console.WriteLine(employee1.Greet(employee2));
    }
}
```

Explanation

1. **Instance Method**:

   - FullName(): An instance method that concatenates the FirstName and LastName properties to produce the full name of the person.

2. **Static Method**:

   - CreateAnonymous(): A static method that creates an instance of Person with default values ("John Doe").

3. **Overriding Methods**:

   - ToString(): Overrides the ToString method to provide a custom string representation of the Person, using the FullName method.

4. **Additional Instance Method**:

   - Greet(Person other): An instance method that generates a greeting message for another Person.

Key Points

- **Methods**: Records can define both instance and static methods, just like classes.
- **Overriding**: Records can override methods such as `ToString`, `Equals`, and `GetHashCode` to customize their behavior.
- **Functionality**: Records can encapsulate functionality and behavior, not just data.

Summary

A `record` in C# can have methods, including instance methods, static methods, and overridden methods. This allows records to encapsulate not only data but also behavior, providing a rich and versatile way to define data-centric types with associated functionality.

Record vs Class

Choosing between a record and a class in C# depends on the specific requirements and intended use of your data structures. Here are some guidelines to help you decide when to use a record over a class:

When to Use a Record

1. **Immutability and Value Semantics**:

    - Use records when you want to create immutable data models with value semantics. Records are designed to be immutable by default, which means their state cannot be modified after they are created.

2. **Data-Centric Models**:

    - Records are ideal for representing data-centric models, such as Data Transfer Objects (DTOs), read-only configurations, or simple data containers where equality is based on the data contained rather than the object identity.

3. **Value-Based Equality**:

    - Use records when you need value-based equality comparisons. Records provide value-based implementations of `Equals` and `GetHashCode` methods, meaning two record instances are considered equal if all their properties have the same values.

4. **Concise Syntax**:

    - Records offer a more concise syntax for defining simple data structures, especially with positional parameters. This makes them easier to read and maintain for straightforward data objects.

When to Use a Class

1. **Mutable Objects**:

    - Use classes when you need mutable objects where the state can change after the object is created. Classes allow you to define setter methods or properties that can be modified.

2. **Behavior-Rich Models**:

- Classes are suitable for behavior-rich models where you need to encapsulate both data and behavior (methods). If your data structure requires complex logic or business rules, a class is more appropriate.

3. **Inheritance and Polymorphism**:

- Use classes when you need to leverage inheritance and polymorphism. Classes support complex inheritance hierarchies and can be used to define abstract base classes or interfaces.

4. **Reference-Based Equality**:

- Classes use reference-based equality by default, which means two instances are considered equal if they reference the same object. This is useful when object identity matters more than the data contained within the object.

Example of a Class

```
public class Person
{
    public string FirstName { get; set; }
    public string LastName { get; set; }

    public void ChangeLastName(string newLastName)
    {
        LastName = newLastName;
    }
}
```

This example defines a class with mutable properties and a method to change the last name, demonstrating how behavior and data can be encapsulated within a class.

Key Differences and Considerations

1. **Immutability**:

    - **Record**: Immutable by default, ideal for data-centric models.
    - **Class**: Mutable by default, suitable for behavior-rich models.

2. **Equality**:

    - **Record**: Value-based equality, comparing property values.
    - **Class**: Reference-based equality, comparing object references.

3. **Syntax**:

    - **Record**: Concise syntax for simple data structures.
    - **Class**: More verbose but flexible for complex logic and behavior.

4. **Inheritance**:

    - **Record**: Supports inheritance but primarily for data structures.
    - **Class**: Fully supports inheritance and polymorphism.

5. **Use Cases**:

    - **Record**: DTOs, immutable data models, configurations.
    - **Class**: Entities with mutable state, business logic, complex inheritance hierarchies.

Summary

- **Use records** for immutable, data-centric models where value-based equality and concise syntax are beneficial.
- **Use classes** for mutable objects, behavior-rich models, and scenarios requiring inheritance and polymorphism.

By understanding the strengths and intended use cases of records and classes, you can choose the appropriate type for your specific requirements.

Records and Thread Safety

Records help with thread safety primarily due to their immutability. When an object is immutable, its state cannot be modified after it is created. This immutability provides several advantages in multi-threaded environments:

Immutability and Thread Safety

1. **No State Changes:**

   - Since records are immutable by default, once a record instance is created, its properties cannot be modified. This means there is no risk of one thread changing the state of an object while another thread is reading it, which eliminates a common source of bugs in multi-threaded applications.

2. **Simplified Reasoning:**

   - Immutability simplifies reasoning about the code because you can be confident that the state of an object will remain consistent throughout its lifetime. There is no need to worry about synchronization issues or race conditions that occur when multiple threads try to modify shared data.

3. **Safe Sharing**:

   - Immutable objects can be freely shared between threads without the need for locks or other synchronization mechanisms. Each thread can safely read the properties of a record without concern for data corruption or inconsistent state.

4. **Functional Programming**:

   - Records promote a functional programming style, where data is transformed rather than modified. This style is inherently more thread-safe because functions operate on copies of data rather than shared mutable state.

Example: Thread-Safe Data Sharing with Records

Consider the following example where multiple threads access and use an immutable record:

```
public record Person(string FirstName, string LastName);

public class Program
{
    public static void Main()
    {
        var person = new Person("John", "Doe");

        Task task1 = Task.Run(() =>
                        DisplayPerson(person));
        Task task2 = Task.Run(() =>
```

```
12                        DisplayPerson(person));
13
14        Task.WaitAll(task1, task2);
15    }
16
17    public static void DisplayPerson(Person person)
18    {
19        Console.WriteLine($"Name: {person.FirstName} 
20                                  {person.LastName}");
21    }
22 }
```

In this example, person is a record, and its properties cannot be modified after it is created. Both task1 and task2 can safely read the properties of person without any risk of one task affecting the other.

Practical Implications

- **Concurrency without Locks:**

    - In scenarios where you need to share data between multiple threads, using immutable records can help you avoid the complexity and overhead of locking mechanisms, making your code simpler and more efficient.

- **Read-Only Data Models:**

    - Records are ideal for read-only data models, such as configuration settings, where the data is initialized once and used by multiple components concurrently.

- **Reduced Bugs:**

    - By eliminating the possibility of state changes, records reduce the likelihood of bugs related to mutable shared state, such as race conditions and data corruption.

Records enhance thread safety through their default immutability, which ensures that the state of an object cannot change after it is created. This immutability makes it safe to share records between multiple threads without the need for synchronization mechanisms, simplifies reasoning about the code, and reduces the likelihood of concurrency-related bugs.

Summary

- The code snippet defines a record `Person` and demonstrates its value-based equality.
- Records provide a convenient way to define immutable data types with value semantics.
- Using records can help ensure that your data models are immutable and that equality checks are based on the values of properties rather than object references.

Init-only Properties - Making Object Initialization More Flexible

Init-only properties introduce a new way to make objects immutable while allowing property values to be set during initialization. They can only be set during object initialization and are read-only thereafter.

Example:

```
public class Product
{
    public string Name { get; init; }
    public decimal Price { get; init; }
}

var product = new Product { Name = "Laptop",
                            Price = 999.99m };
// product.Name = "Tablet"; // Compiler error
// Init-only property can only be assigned
// during initialization
Console.WriteLine($"{product.Name}, {product.Price}");
```

Top-level Statements - Simplifying Small Programs and Scripts

Top-level statements in C# 9.0 simplify the entry point of applications, reducing the boilerplate code typically associated with small programs and scripts.

Example:

```
// This is the entire content of a C# file
// with top-level statements
Console.WriteLine("Hello, World!");
```

Top-level statements in C# 9.0 indeed simplify the entry point of applications, especially for small programs and scripts. However, there are some limitations and considerations to keep in mind when using this feature. Here's an overview of what you can and can't do with top-level statements, along with some additional details:

What You Can Do

1. **Simplify Entry Point**: Top-level statements allow you to write code directly at the root level of a file without needing to define a Main method, reducing boilerplate.

```
// This is the entire content of a C# file with
// top-level statements
Console.WriteLine("Hello, World!");
```

2. **Access Command-Line Arguments**: You can access command-line arguments using the args array.

```
if (args.Length > 0)
{
    Console.WriteLine($"Hello, {args[0]}!");
}
else
{
    Console.WriteLine("Hello, World!");
}
```

3. **Define Local Functions**: You can define local functions within top-level statements.

```
Console.WriteLine("Hello, World!");

void PrintMessage(string message)
{
    Console.WriteLine(message);
}

PrintMessage("This is a local function.");
```

4. **Use Await**: You can use await directly in top-level statements if you need to perform asynchronous operations.

```
using System.Net.Http;

HttpClient client = new HttpClient();
string response = await client.GetStringAsync(
                    "https://api.github.com");
Console.WriteLine(response);
```

What You Can't Do

1. **Multiple Top-Level Files**: You can't have multiple files with top-level statements in the same project. Only one file can contain top-level statements, and it implicitly defines the entry point.
2. **Class Definitions in the Same File**: While you can define local functions and use variables, you can't define new classes, structs, or records within the same file as top-level statements. Those must be in separate files or outside the scope of the top-level statements.

```
// Invalid:
// Top-level statements here

//public class MyClass
//{
//     // Class definition
//}
```

3. **Multiple Entry Points**: As with traditional Main methods, you can't define multiple entry points in a single project. If you have a Main method defined elsewhere, you can't use top-level statements in the same project.
4. **Namespaces and Usings**: While you can still use namespaces and using directives, they need to be declared before the top-level statements. You can't place them inline within the top-level code.

```
1    using System;
2
3    // Top-level statements start here
4    Console.WriteLine("Hello, World!");
```

5. **Explicit Main Method Parameters**: While you can access command-line arguments via the args array, you can't explicitly declare a Main method with parameters in a file with top-level statements.
6. **Attributes on Main**: You can't apply attributes directly to the implicit Main method created by top-level statements. Attributes that need to be applied to the Main method must be used in a traditional Main method definition.

Additional Considerations

- **Variable Scope**: Variables declared in top-level statements have a scope similar to variables declared in the Main method of a traditional C# program. They are scoped to the file and can be accessed by any code within the same file.
- **Application Structure**: For larger applications, top-level statements might not be the best choice. They are ideal for small scripts, quick prototypes, and educational purposes but might lead to less clear code organization in larger projects.

Example of Combined Features

Here's an example that combines several features of top-level statements:

```csharp
using System;
using System.Net.Http;
using System.Threading.Tasks;

Console.WriteLine("Starting program...");

if (args.Length > 0)
{
    Console.WriteLine($"Argument received: {args[0]}");
}

await FetchDataFromApiAsync();

void PrintMessage(string message)
{
    Console.WriteLine(message);
}

async Task FetchDataFromApiAsync()
{
    HttpClient client = new HttpClient();
    string response = await client.GetStringAsync(
                    "https://api.github.com");
    // Print only the first 100 characters
    PrintMessage(response.Substring(0, 100));
}
```

This example demonstrates how you can use `await`, define local functions, and access command-line arguments within top-level statements.

Summary

Top-level statements in C# 9.0 simplify the entry point of applications and are particularly useful for small programs and scripts.

However, they come with some limitations, such as the inability to have multiple top-level files, define classes within the same file, or apply attributes to the implicit Main method. Understanding these constraints will help you decide when to use top-level statements effectively.

Pattern Matching Enhancements: Relational Patterns, Logical Patterns

C# 9.0 expanded pattern matching capabilities to include relational and logical patterns, allowing for more expressive and concise conditional logic.

Relational Patterns Example:

```
int age = 34;
string lifeStage = age switch
{
    < 13 => "Child",
    < 20 => "Teenager",
    < 60 => "Adult",
    _ => "Senior"
};
Console.WriteLine(lifeStage); // Output: Adult
```

Logical Patterns Example:

```
bool isLetter(char c) => c switch
{
    >= 'a' and <= 'z' or >= 'A' and <= 'Z' => true,
    _ => false
};
Console.WriteLine(isLetter('x')); // Output: True
```

Native Sized Integers for Performance-Critical Scenarios

Native sized integers (nint and nuint) were introduced to provide seamless interoperability with native code without having to use IntPtr.

Example:

```
nint index = 5;
nuint length = 10;

Console.WriteLine($"Index: {index}, Length: {length}");
```

A More Detailed Example of nint and nuint.

IntPtr and nint are similar in that they both represent platform-specific integer types, but they are used in different contexts and have different characteristics. Here's a comparison and an example to clarify their usage:

Differences Between IntPtr and nint

- **IntPtr:**

- Represents a platform-specific pointer or handle.
- Can be used to store a pointer or handle value.
- Provides methods for pointer arithmetic and conversions.
- Commonly used in interop scenarios with unmanaged code (e.g., P/Invoke).

- **nint**:

    - Represents a platform-specific signed integer.
    - Primarily used for arithmetic operations that need to match the platform's native integer size.
    - Does not inherently represent a pointer but can be used in scenarios where platform-specific integer arithmetic is required.

Example Using `nint` for Memory Operations

Using nint and nuint ensures we use the correct byte increment size when we want to step through memory. Here's an example using IntPtr and `nint` to manipulate memory:

```
using System;
using System.Runtime.InteropServices;

public class Program
{
    public static void Main()
    {
        // Allocate 100 bytes of unmanaged memory
        nuint size = 100;
        IntPtr memory = Marshal.AllocHGlobal((int)size);

        try
```

```csharp
        {
            // Cast IntPtr to nint for arithmetic
            // operations
            nint baseAddress = (nint)memory;

            // Write values to the allocated memory
            for (nuint i = 0; i < size; i++)
            {
                Marshal.WriteByte(
                    (IntPtr)(baseAddress + (nint)i),
                    (byte)(i % 256));
            }

            // Read a value from a specific memory
            // location
            nint offset = 50; // Go to the 50th byte
            byte value = Marshal.ReadByte(
                (IntPtr)(baseAddress + offset));

            Console.WriteLine(
                $"Value at offset {offset}: {value}");
        }
        finally
        {
            // Free the allocated memory
            Marshal.FreeHGlobal(memory);
        }
    }
}
```

Explanation

1. **Allocating Unmanaged Memory**:

- `Marshal.AllocHGlobal` allocates a block of unmanaged memory on the heap.

2. **Casting IntPtr to nint:**

    - The base address of the allocated memory is obtained as an `IntPtr` and cast to `nint` for arithmetic operations.

3. **Writing to Memory:**

    - The loop writes byte values to the allocated memory block. Arithmetic is performed using `nint` for the base address and the index.

4. **Reading from a Specific Memory Location:**

    - The `Marshal.ReadByte` method reads a byte value from a specific offset within the allocated memory block, using `nint` for the offset calculation.

5. **Freeing Unmanaged Memory:**

    - `Marshal.FreeHGlobal` is called in a `finally` block to free the allocated memory, preventing leaks.

Key Points

- **Interop Scenarios:** `IntPtr` is typically used in interop scenarios, as it directly represents a pointer or handle.
- **Arithmetic Operations:** `nint` is useful for performing platform-specific arithmetic operations but does not inherently represent a pointer.

By understanding the differences and appropriate contexts for IntPtr and nint, you can use them effectively in your applications. In scenarios involving direct pointer manipulation or interop with unmanaged code, IntPtr remains the more appropriate choice.

C# 9.0 introduces a suite of features that refine the language's syntax and expand its capabilities, especially concerning data handling and pattern matching. Records streamline the definition of immutable types with value-based equality. Init-only properties enhance the immutability pattern common in modern C#. Top-level statements reduce the friction of writing small utilities or scripts by removing unnecessary boilerplate. Enhanced pattern matching adds powerful new syntax for expressing complex conditions succinctly. Native sized integers optimize performance when interfacing with system calls or native libraries. Together, these features significantly elevate the power and simplicity of C# programming.

Chapter 8: C# 10.0 - Further Refinements and Global Usings

C# 10.0 continues the evolution of the language, introducing features that simplify coding practices, enhance performance, and streamline code structure. This chapter discusses these new additions, providing clear examples to illustrate how each feature can be utilized in real-world scenarios.

Global Using Directives - Simplifying Project-wide Imports

Global using directives allow developers to specify namespace imports that are applied across all files in a project, reducing redundancy and clutter in individual files.

Example:

```
// In a GlobalUsings.cs file or at the top of any C# file
global using System;
global using System.Collections.Generic;

// Now, every file in the project can use types from
// System and System.Collections.Generic without
// declaring them
```

File-Scoped Namespaces - Reducing Nesting and Improving Readability

File-scoped namespaces reduce the amount of nesting in files, which improves readability by decreasing the indent level required for most of the code.

Example:

```
// Before C# 10.0
namespace MyApplication.Models
{
    public class Product
    {
        public int Id { get; set; }
        public string Name { get; set; }
    }
}

// With C# 10.0
namespace MyApplication.Models;

public class Product
{
    public int Id { get; set; }
    public string Name { get; set; }
}
```

Record Structs - Combining the Benefits of Records and Structs

Record structs combine the immutability and value-based equality of records with the value-type semantics of structs, offering an efficient way to represent lightweight data structures.

Example:

```
public record struct Point(int X, int Y);

var p1 = new Point(1, 2);
var p2 = new Point(1, 2);
Console.WriteLine(p1 == p2); // Output: True
```

record struct VS. struct

Both record struct and struct in C# are value types, but they are used for different purposes and have distinct characteristics. Here's a comparison of record struct and struct:

Struct

A struct in C# is a value type primarily used for small, lightweight data structures. It is typically mutable and focuses on performance by avoiding heap allocations.

Characteristics of struct:

1. **Value Type:**

    - Allocated on the stack (or inline in arrays), leading to lower memory overhead and better performance in certain scenarios.

2. **Mutability:**

    - Structs are mutable by default, which means their fields and properties can be changed after the instance is created.

3. **Equality:**

    - Structs use value-based equality for fields by default but do not automatically provide deep value-based equality. You can override `Equals` and `GetHashCode` if needed.

4. **Use Cases:**

    - Best suited for small data structures, mathematical types (like `Point`, `Vector`), and scenarios where performance and memory efficiency are critical.

5. **Inheritance:**

    - Structs do not support inheritance. They can implement interfaces but cannot inherit from other structs or classes.

Example of a `struct`:

```
public struct Point
{
    public int X { get; set; }
    public int Y { get; set; }

    public Point(int x, int y)
    {
        X = x;
        Y = y;
    }

    public double DistanceTo(Point other)
    {
        int dx = X - other.X;
        int dy = Y - other.Y;
```

```
16          return Math.Sqrt(dx * dx + dy * dy);
17      }
18  }
```

`record struct`

A `record struct` combines the benefits of a `struct` with the features of records, such as immutability and built-in value-based equality.

Characteristics of `record struct`:

1. **Value Type:**

    - Like regular structs, record structs are allocated on the stack, leading to similar performance benefits.

2. **Immutability:**

    - Record structs are immutable by default, meaning their state cannot be modified after they are created. This immutability ensures that the data remains consistent and thread-safe.

3. **Equality:**

    - Record structs provide built-in value-based equality, meaning the `Equals` and `GetHashCode` methods are automatically generated to compare the values of the properties.

4. **Concise Syntax:**

    - Record structs offer a concise syntax for defining data structures with positional parameters and deconstructors.

5. **Use Cases**:

    - Ideal for small, immutable data structures that benefit from value semantics, such as DTOs and simple value objects.

6. **Inheritance**:

    - Record structs do not support inheritance, similar to regular structs. They can implement interfaces but cannot inherit from other structs or classes.

Example of a `record struct`:

```
public readonly record struct Point(int X, int Y)
{
    public double DistanceTo(Point other)
    {
        int dx = X - other.X;
        int dy = Y - other.Y;
        return Math.Sqrt(dx * dx + dy * dy);
    }
}
```

Key Differences

1. **Immutability**:

    - **Struct**: Mutable by default. You need to explicitly make fields or properties read-only if you want immutability.
    - **Record Struct**: Immutable by default, promoting a functional programming style.

2. **Equality**:

- **Struct**: Uses default value-based equality but does not automatically provide deep equality. Custom implementation may be needed.
- **Record Struct**: Provides built-in value-based equality, comparing the values of properties automatically.

3. **Syntax**:

   - **Struct**: Requires more verbose syntax for defining properties, constructors, and methods.
   - **Record Struct**: Offers a concise syntax with positional parameters and automatic deconstruction.

4. **Typical Use Cases**:

   - **Struct**: Small, performance-critical data structures where mutability is acceptable or required.
   - **Record Struct**: Small, immutable data structures where value-based equality and immutability are important.

Summary

- **Use `struct`**: When you need a small, mutable value type for performance-critical scenarios, such as mathematical types or small data structures where memory efficiency is key.
- **Use `record struct`**: When you need a small, immutable value type with built-in value-based equality, typically for data-centric models or scenarios where immutability and thread safety are important.

By understanding these differences, you can choose the appropriate type for your specific needs, leveraging the strengths of each.

Improved Lambda Expressions and Attributes on Lambda Expressions

C# 10.0 enhances lambda expressions by supporting attributes and natural type inference, which allows for more concise and powerful lambda definitions.

Example:

```
Func<int, int> square =
            [System.Diagnostics.CodeAnalysis.NotNull]
            (int x) => x * x;
Console.WriteLine(square(5)); // Output: 25

// Lambda with explicit return type
var doubler = (int x) => x * 2;
Console.WriteLine(doubler(4)); // Output: 8
```

In our doubler example, we can infer that the return type is an integer because the parameter passed into the lambda is an integer and we are multiplying by an integer 2.

Constant Interpolated Strings - Enhancing Performance in String Manipulations

Constant interpolated strings in C# 10.0 are evaluated at compile time, thus eliminating runtime overhead associated with string interpolation in constant expressions.

Example:

```
const string name = "World";
const string greeting = $"Hello, {name}"; // This is
                                          // evaluated at
                                          // compile-time in
                                          // C# 10.0

Console.WriteLine(greeting); // Output: Hello, World
```

Review of Interpolated Strings

Interpolated strings, introduced in C# 6.0, provide a convenient way to embed expressions within string literals. This feature enhances code readability and maintainability by allowing inline expression evaluation and formatting directly within the string.

Basic Usage

Interpolated strings are defined using the $ symbol before the string literal. Expressions to be embedded are enclosed within curly braces {}.

Adding Formatting

You can include format specifiers within the curly braces to control the format of the embedded expressions. This is useful for formatting dates, numbers, and other data types.

Example with Date Formatting

Chapter 8: C# 10.0 - Further Refinements and Global Usings

```csharp
DateTime date = DateTime.Now;
string formattedDate = $"Today's date is
                       {date:MM/dd/yyyy}";
Console.WriteLine(formattedDate);
// Output: "Today's date is 06/08/2024"
// (depending on the current date)
```

Example with Number Formatting

```csharp
double number = 1234.5678;
string formattedNumber = $"Formatted number: {number:F2}";
Console.WriteLine(formattedNumber);
// Output: "Formatted number: 1234.57"
```

Advanced Formatting

You can use standard .NET format specifiers to control the output of various data types:

- **Numeric Formats**:

    - C or c: Currency
    - D or d: Decimal
    - E or e: Exponential (scientific) notation
    - F or f: Fixed-point
    - G or g: General
    - N or n: Number
    - P or p: Percent
    - X or x: Hexadecimal

Example with Multiple Formats

```
int value = 255;
string hexValue = $"Hexadecimal: {value:X}";
string decimalValue = $"Decimal: {value:D}";
string currencyValue = $"Currency: {value:C}";
Console.WriteLine(hexValue);        // Output:
                                    // "Hexadecimal: FF"
Console.WriteLine(decimalValue);    // Output: "Decimal:
                                    //              255"
Console.WriteLine(currencyValue);   // Output: "Currency:
                                    //          $255.00"
```

Constant Interpolated Strings

C# 10.0 introduced **constant** interpolated strings, which are evaluated at compile time. This feature eliminates runtime overhead associated with string interpolation in constant expressions.

However, this feature is limited to scenarios where all the components of the interpolated string are constants and can be fully evaluated at compile time. Unfortunately, format specifiers (like :X, :D, and :C) cannot be used in constant interpolated strings.

Correct Usage of Constant Interpolated Strings

While you can use constant interpolated strings for simple expressions, they do not support format specifiers. Here is what you can and can't do with constant interpolated strings:

What You Can Do

You can use constant interpolated strings with simple constant values:

Chapter 8: C# 10.0 - Further Refinements and Global Usings

```
const string name = "World";

// This is evaluated at compile-time
const string greeting = $"Hello, {name}";
```

What You Can't Do

You can't use format specifiers with constant interpolated strings because they require runtime evaluation:

```
const int value = 255;
// This will not compile
const string hexValue = $"Hexadecimal: {value:X}";
// This will not compile
const string decimalValue = $"Decimal: {value:D}";
// This will not compile
const string currencyValue = $"Currency: {value:C}";
```

Alternative Approach

To use formatting with interpolated strings, you must use `readonly` fields instead of `const`:

Example Using Readonly Fields

```csharp
using System;

internal class InterpolatedStringsExample
{
    const int value = 255;
    readonly string hexValue = $"Hexadecimal: {value:X}";
    readonly string decimalValue = $"Decimal: {value:D}";
    readonly string currencyValue =
                        $"Currency: {value:C}";

    public InterpolatedStringsExample()
    {
        // Initialization of readonly fields
        hexValue = $"Hexadecimal: {value:X}";
        decimalValue = $"Decimal: {value:D}";
        currencyValue = $"Currency: {value:C}";
    }

    public void DisplayInterpolatedString()
    {
        Console.WriteLine(hexValue); // Output:
                                     // "Hexadecimal: FF"
        Console.WriteLine(decimalValue); // Output:
                                         // "Decimal: 255"
        Console.WriteLine(currencyValue); // Output:
                                          // "Currency:
                                          //  $255.00"
    }
}

public class Program
{
    public static void Main()
    {
        var example = new InterpolatedStringsExample();
```

```
        example.DisplayInterpolatedString();
    }
}
```

Summary

- **Constant Interpolated Strings**: Can be used when all components are constants and no format specifiers are needed.
- **Readonly Fields**: Use `readonly` fields for interpolated strings that require format specifiers or other runtime evaluations.

C# 10.0 introduces a set of features that further refine the language, making it more powerful and easier to use. Global using directives simplify how namespaces are managed across projects. File-scoped namespaces reduce unnecessary code nesting, making files cleaner and easier to read. Record structs provide a new way to model data with both the efficiency of structs and the benefits of records. Improvements to lambda expressions and the introduction of constant interpolated strings enhance the language's capabilities in functional programming and performance-critical applications. By adopting these features, developers can write more efficient, readable, and maintainable C# code.

Chapter 9: C# 11.0 - Focused on Safety and Clarity

C# 11.0 continues the trend of evolving the language to enhance safety, reduce potential errors, and improve the clarity of code. This chapter delves into several new features introduced in this version, explaining their utility and providing examples to demonstrate their practical applications.

List Patterns - Enhancing Pattern Matching with Collections

List patterns extend the capabilities of pattern matching to effectively deal with collections. This allows developers to match sequences against patterns directly within collection types such as arrays or lists.

Example:

```
int[] numbers = { 1, 2, 3, 4, 5 };

if (numbers is [1, 2, 3, ..])
{
    Console.WriteLine("The array starts with 1, 2, 3.");
}
// Output: The array starts with 1, 2, 3.
```

In this example, the `is` pattern checks if the array starts with the numbers 1, 2, 3 followed by any sequence (indicated by ..), which is a list pattern checking for a specific start of the sequence.

List patterns in C# provide powerful capabilities for pattern matching with collections, such as arrays and lists. This feature allows you to match sequences against patterns directly within these collection types. Here are some more examples demonstrating how to use list patterns effectively:

Matching Exact Sequences

You can match an exact sequence of elements in a list or array:

```
int[] numbers = { 1, 2, 3, 4, 5 };

if (numbers is [1, 2, 3, 4, 5])
{
    Console.WriteLine(
        "The array is exactly [1, 2, 3, 4, 5].");
}
// Output: The array is exactly [1, 2, 3, 4, 5].
```

Matching Sequences with Wildcards

You can use the _ wildcard to match any single element:

```
int[] numbers = { 1, 2, 3, 4, 5 };

if (numbers is [1, _, 3, _, 5])
{
    Console.WriteLine(
        "The array matches the pattern [1, _, 3, _, 5].");
}
// Output: The array matches the pattern [1, _, 3, _, 5].
```

Matching Sequences with Ranges

You can use the .. pattern to match any sequence of elements:

```
int[] numbers = { 1, 2, 3, 4, 5 };

if (numbers is [1, 2, ..])
{
    Console.WriteLine("The array starts with [1, 2].");
}
// Output: The array starts with [1, 2].
```

Matching Sequences with Ranges and Specific End

You can combine specific elements with the .. pattern to match sequences with specific ends:

```
int[] numbers = { 1, 2, 3, 4, 5 };

if (numbers is [.., 4, 5])
{
    Console.WriteLine("The array ends with [4, 5].");
}
// Output: The array ends with [4, 5].
```

Matching Nested Patterns

You can use nested patterns within list patterns to match complex structures:

```
int[][] nestedNumbers = { new int[] { 1, 2 }, new int[]
                        { 3, 4 }, new int[] { 5, 6 } };

if (nestedNumbers is [ [1, 2], [3, 4], .. ])
{
    Console.WriteLine(
        "The nested array starts with [1, 2] and [3, 4].
        ");
}
// Output: The nested array starts with [1, 2] and [3, 4].
```

Using List Patterns with Lists

List patterns also work with List<T> and other collection types:

```csharp
List<int> numberList = new List<int> { 1, 2, 3, 4, 5 };

if (numberList is [1, 2, ..])
{
    Console.WriteLine("The list starts with [1, 2].");
}
// Output: The list starts with [1, 2].
```

Combining Patterns with Conditions

You can combine list patterns with additional conditions:

```csharp
int[] numbers = { 1, 2, 3, 4, 5 };

if (numbers is [1, 2, 3, .. var rest] && rest.Length == 2)
{
    Console.WriteLine(
        "The array starts with [1, 2, 3] and has exactly
        2 more elements.");
}
// Output: The array starts with [1, 2, 3]
// and has exactly 2 more elements.
```

Summary

List patterns in C# extend the capabilities of pattern matching to collections, allowing developers to write more expressive and concise code. These examples demonstrate various ways to leverage list patterns, from matching exact sequences and wildcards to nested patterns and additional conditions. By utilizing these patterns, you can handle collections more effectively in your C# programs.

Required Properties - Ensuring Object Initialization Integrity

C# 11.0 introduces required properties, which ensure that certain properties must be initialized when an object is created. This is particularly useful for non-nullable reference types and ensuring data integrity right upon object construction.

Example:

```
public class Person
{
    public required string Name { get; set; }
    public required int Age { get; set; }
}

// Usage

// Valid
var person = new Person { Name = "John", Age = 30 };

// var invalidPerson = new Person { Name = "Jane" };
// Compile-time error, Age is required
```

This feature prevents objects from being instantiated without initializing all required properties, ensuring that objects are always in a valid state.

Raw String Literals - Simplifying the Representation of Strings

Raw string literals in C# 11.0 provide a way to write strings that preserve whitespace, newlines, and special characters like backslashes without the need for escaping. This feature is especially useful for writing file paths, JSON, XML, HTML, regular expressions, and multi-line strings.

Example:

```
string path = """C:\Users\Example\Documents\Project""";
Console.WriteLine(path);
// Output: C:\Users\Example\Documents\Project
```

Raw string literals use triple quotes (`"""`) to start and end the string, allowing for unescaped backslashes and clearer string content.

Key Features of Raw String Literals

1. **Triple Quotes (`"""`):**

    - Raw string literals are enclosed in triple quotes (`"""`), allowing the content inside to be preserved exactly as written, without the need for escape sequences.

2. **Multi-line Support:**

    - Raw string literals can span multiple lines, preserving the exact layout and indentation.

3. **Embedding Quotes:**

    - You can include quotes and triple quotes within a raw string literal by adjusting the number of starting and ending quotes.

Examples of Raw String Literals

File Paths

```
string path = """C:\Users\Example\Documents\Project""";
Console.WriteLine(path);
// Output: C:\Users\Example\Documents\Project
```

Multi-line Strings

```
string multiLine = """
This is a multi-line
raw string literal that preserves
    indentation and line breaks.
""";
Console.WriteLine(multiLine);
// Output:
// This is a multi-line
// raw string literal that preserves
//     indentation and line breaks.
```

JSON

```
string json = """
{
    "name": "John Doe",
    "age": 30,
    "isEmployed": true,
    "address": {
        "street": "123 Main St",
        "city": "Anytown",
        "state": "CA"
    }
}
""";
Console.WriteLine(json);
// Output:
// {
```

```
16  //      "name": "John Doe",
17  //      "age": 30,
18  //      "isEmployed": true,
19  //      "address": {
20  //          "street": "123 Main St",
21  //          "city": "Anytown",
22  //          "state": "CA"
23  //      }
24  // }
```

HTML

```
1   string html = """
2   <!DOCTYPE html>
3   <html>
4   <head>
5       <title>Raw String Literal Example</title>
6   </head>
7   <body>
8       <h1>Hello, World!</h1>
9   </body>
10  </html>
11  """;
12  Console.WriteLine(html);
13  // Output:
14  // <!DOCTYPE html>
15  // <html>
16  // <head>
17  //     <title>Raw String Literal Example</title>
18  // </head>
19  // <body>
20  //     <h1>Hello, World!</h1>
21  // </body>
22  // </html>
```

Regular Expressions

```csharp
string regex = """
^\d{4}-\d{2}-\d{2}$
""";
Console.WriteLine(regex);
// Output: ^\d{4}-\d{2}-\d{2}$
```

Embedding Quotes

To include double or triple quotes within a raw string literal, you adjust the number of starting and ending quotes:

```csharp
string withQuotes =
    """"Here is a "quoted" text inside a raw string
    literal"""";
Console.WriteLine(withQuotes);
// Output: Here is a "quoted" text inside a
// raw string literal
```

Advantages of Raw String Literals

1. **Readability**: Raw string literals improve readability by avoiding the need for escape sequences, making the string content appear as it does in the source code.
2. **Maintenance**: Easier to maintain strings that involve multiple lines or special characters, such as file paths, regular expressions, and markup languages.
3. **Accuracy**: Preserves the exact formatting, including whitespace and newlines, which is particularly useful for code generation, templates, and embedded scripts.

Summary

Raw string literals in C# 11.0 provide a powerful way to handle complex string content without escaping, preserving the exact layout and formatting. They enhance readability and maintainability for strings that contain special characters, multi-line text, and embedded markup or code. By using triple quotes and allowing embedded quotes, raw string literals offer a versatile solution for various scenarios in C# programming.

Improved Definite Assignment - Reducing Nullability Warnings

C# 11.0 improves the definite assignment rules, particularly around nullable reference types, to reduce unnecessary compiler warnings about the potential use of uninitialized non-nullable variables.

Example:

```
string? input = Console.ReadLine();
if (input is not null)
{
    // The compiler understands 'input' is
    // definitely not null here.
    Console.WriteLine(input.Length);
}
```

The improvements in definite assignment checking ensure that the compiler more accurately tracks variables through control flow, recognizing when a nullable reference has been definitively assigned a non-null value.

Async Method Builder Overriding - Customizing Task-Like Return Types

C# 11.0 introduces the capability to override the async method builder for asynchronous methods. This feature allows developers to customize how task-like types are handled, enabling optimizations or behaviors specific to their applications.

Example:

```
using System.Runtime.CompilerServices;
using System.Threading.Tasks;

[AsyncMethodBuilder(typeof(CustomTaskMethodBuilder))]
public class CustomTask
{
    // Custom implementation details here
}

public class CustomTaskMethodBuilder
{
    public static CustomTaskMethodBuilder Create() =>
                    new CustomTaskMethodBuilder();

    // Implementation details for building the task
}

// Usage
public async CustomTask ProcessDataAsync()
{
    await Task.Delay(1000);   // Simulate asynchronous
                              // operation
    Console.WriteLine("Data processed");
}
```

This allows for sophisticated control over the async execution environment, suitable for applications requiring specific performance characteristics or behaviors from their asynchronous operations.

Complete Example

To run this example successfully, you'll need to implement a custom async method builder for your `CustomTask`. This involves defining how the async state machine is created, started, awaited, and completed. This is an advanced feature of C# and typically used in very specific scenarios where custom behavior for async operations is required.

Here is a complete example demonstrating how to set up and use a custom async method builder with a custom task type:

Step-by-Step Implementation

1. **Define the `CustomTask` Class:**

   - The custom task type that your async methods will return.

2. **Define the `CustomTaskMethodBuilder` Class:**

   - The custom method builder that handles the async state machine for the custom task type.

Complete Code Example

```csharp
using System;
using System.Runtime.CompilerServices;
using System.Threading.Tasks;

// Custom Task Type
[AsyncMethodBuilder(typeof(CustomTaskMethodBuilder))]
public class CustomTask
{
    public CustomTaskAwaiter GetAwaiter() =>
                            new CustomTaskAwaiter();

    public class CustomTaskAwaiter : INotifyCompletion
    {
        public bool IsCompleted => true;

        public void GetResult() { }

        public void OnCompleted(Action continuation) =>
                                        continuation();
    }
}

// Custom Task Method Builder
public class CustomTaskMethodBuilder
{
    private TaskCompletionSource<object?> _tcs =
            new TaskCompletionSource<object?>();

    public static CustomTaskMethodBuilder Create() =>
            new CustomTaskMethodBuilder();

    public CustomTask Task => new CustomTask();

    public void SetResult() => _tcs.SetResult(null);
```

```csharp
    public void SetException(Exception exception) =>
        _tcs.SetException(exception);

    public void AwaitOnCompleted<TAwaiter, TStateMachine>
    (ref TAwaiter awaiter, ref TStateMachine stateMachine)
        where TAwaiter : INotifyCompletion
        where TStateMachine : IAsyncStateMachine
    {
        awaiter.OnCompleted(stateMachine.MoveNext);
    }

    public void AwaitUnsafeOnCompleted<TAwaiter,
            TStateMachine>(ref TAwaiter awaiter,
                ref TStateMachine stateMachine)
        where TAwaiter : ICriticalNotifyCompletion
        where TStateMachine : IAsyncStateMachine
    {
        awaiter.OnCompleted(stateMachine.MoveNext);
    }

    public void Start<TStateMachine>(
                    ref TStateMachine stateMachine)
        where TStateMachine : IAsyncStateMachine
    {
        stateMachine.MoveNext();
    }

    public void SetStateMachine(
        IAsyncStateMachine stateMachine) { }
}

// Usage
public class Program
{
    public static async CustomTask ProcessDataAsync()
```

```
    {
        await Task.Delay(1000);    // Simulate
                                   // asynchronous operation
        Console.WriteLine("Data processed");
    }

    public static void Main()
    {
        var task = ProcessDataAsync();
        task.GetAwaiter().GetResult();   // To keep the
                                         // console open until
                                         // async operation
                                         // completes
    }
}
```

Explanation

1. **CustomTask Class:**

   - The `CustomTask` class is marked with the `[AsyncMethodBuilder]` attribute to specify the custom method builder.
   - It includes a nested `CustomTaskAwaiter` class that implements the `INotifyCompletion` interface.

2. **CustomTaskMethodBuilder Class:**

   - The `CustomTaskMethodBuilder` class handles the creation and management of the async state machine.
   - The `Create` method initializes the method builder.
   - The `Task` property returns a new instance of `CustomTask`.
   - The `SetResult`, `SetException`, `AwaitOnCompleted`, `AwaitUnsafeOnCompleted`, `Start`, and `SetStateMachine` methods are implemented to manage the state of the async operation.

3. **Usage:**

    - The `ProcessDataAsync` method demonstrates the usage of the custom async method builder and custom task type.
    - The `Main` method calls `ProcessDataAsync` and uses `GetAwaiter().GetResult()` to wait for the async operation to complete.

This example demonstrates the basic setup for using custom async method builders in C#. For more complex scenarios, you may need to extend the `CustomTask` and `CustomTaskMethodBuilder` classes with additional functionality.

C# 11.0 brings forward features that enhance the safety, clarity, and flexibility of the language. From ensuring data integrity with required properties to simplifying how developers handle strings with raw literals, each feature contributes to making C# a more robust and developer-friendly language. The introduction of list patterns and enhanced async capabilities further demonstrates the language's commitment to modern software development paradigms.

Chapter 10: C# 12.0 - The Latest Innovations

C# 12.0 introduces several features that further refine and enhance the language, adding syntactical sugar, increasing performance options, and offering more powerful tools for developers to manage code complexity and expressiveness. This chapter explores these new features, demonstrating their utility through practical examples.

Primary Constructors

Primary constructors in C# 12.0 simplify class and struct definition by allowing parameters to be defined directly in the type declaration, automatically assigning them to properties.

Example:

```
public class Person(string firstName, string lastName)
{
    public string FirstName { get; } = firstName;
    public string LastName { get; } = lastName;
}

// Usage
var person = new Person("John", "Doe");
Console.WriteLine(
    $"{person.FirstName} {person.LastName}");
```

In this example, `Person` class declares its constructor parameters right in the class declaration, simplifying property initialization.

Collection Expressions

Collection expressions provide a more concise way to initialize collections based on existing sequences, making it easier to define and manipulate data sets. Note, you still need to be explicit about the collection type, var won't work.

Simple Example:

```
IList<int> numbers = [1, 2, 3, 4]; // collection
                                   //  expression
foreach (var number in numbers)
{
    Console.Write($"{number}, ");  // output:
}                                  // 1, 2, 3, 4,
```

Using the spread operator

```
int[] greaterValues = [5, 6];
int[] lesserValues = [-1,0];
int[] largerList = [..lesserValues, ..numbers, ..
                                    greaterValues, 7];

foreach (var number in largerList)
{
    Console.Write($"{number}, ");  // output:
}
```

Using the Spread Operator in C# 12.0 Collection Expressions

In C# 12.0, the spread operator (..) can be used within collection expressions to include the elements of other collections, creating more flexible and concise initialization of arrays and lists.

Example

```csharp
int[] greaterValues = { 5, 6 };
int[] lesserValues = { -1, 0 };
int[] numbers = { 1, 2, 3, 4 };
int[] largerList = [..lesserValues, ..numbers,
                    ..greaterValues, 7];

foreach (var number in largerList)
{
    Console.Write($"{number}, ");
}
// Output: -1, 0, 1, 2, 3, 4, 5, 6, 7,
```

Explanation

1. **Initial Arrays:**

   - greaterValues is initialized with [5, 6].
   - lesserValues is initialized with [-1, 0].
   - numbers is initialized with [1, 2, 3, 4].

2. **Combining Arrays with Spread Operator:**

   - largerList is created using the spread operator .. to include elements from lesserValues, numbers, and greaterValues.
   - The spread operator expands each of the three arrays into the new array, followed by the individual element 7.

Output

When iterating over `largerList`, the output will be:

```
-1, 0, 1, 2, 3, 4, 5, 6, 7,
```

This demonstrates how the spread operator simplifies the process of combining arrays and adding new elements in a concise and readable manner.

Ref Readonly Parameters

Ref readonly parameters enhance performance by allowing methods to return large structures or data without copying while ensuring they cannot be modified by the callee.

Example:

```csharp
public struct LargeData
{
    public readonly long[] Data;
    public LargeData(long[] data) => Data = data;
}

public void ProcessData(ref readonly LargeData data)
{
    // data.Data[0] = 123; // This would be an error:
    // cannot assign to a member of a readonly variable
    Console.WriteLine(data.Data.Length);
}

// Usage
var largeData = new LargeData(new long[1000000]);
ProcessData(ref largeData);
```

Default Lambda Parameters

C# 12.0 allows lambda expressions to define default values for parameters, offering greater flexibility and reducing boilerplate code when dealing with delegate-based APIs. In the example below y is set to a default value to 1 in the add function.

Example:

```
var incrementValue =
    (int source, int increment = 3) =>
                        source + increment;
Console.WriteLine(incrementValue(5)); // output 8
```

Alias Any Type

The ability to alias any type improves readability and simplifies code where types have long or complicated names.

Example:

```
//ProjectMatrix alias for Dictionary -
// placed at top of file
using ProjectMatrix = System.Collections.Generic.
    Dictionary<int, System.Collections.Generic.
                            List<string>>;

ProjectMatrix matrix = new ProjectMatrix();
matrix.Add(1, new List<string> { "Hello", "World" });
Console.WriteLine(matrix[1][0]); // Output: HELLO
```

Inline Arrays

Inline arrays simplify the syntax for array creation, making it clearer and more concise. The following example creates a 10 element integer array with the first element being a value of 15.

Example:

```
[System.Runtime.CompilerServices.InlineArray(10)]
public struct Buffer
{
    private int _element0;

    public Buffer()
    {
        _element0 = 15;
        // compiler automatically fills in
        // the other 9 elements with default values
    }
}

Buffer buffer = new Buffer();

buffer[8] = 45;
// Simulating the array access
// (for demonstration purposes)
Console.WriteLine()
for (int i = 0; i < 10; i++)
{
    Console.Write($"{i}:{buffer[i]}, ");
}
// Output:
// 0:15, 1:0, 2:0, 3:0, 4:0, 5:0, 6:0, 7:0, 8:45, 9:0,
```

Experimental Attribute

The Experimental attribute can be used to mark certain features or methods in your codebase that are not finalized, warning other developers or users of the API about the experimental status.

Example:

```
1  [Experimental("EXP041")]
2  public void TestFeature()
3  {
4    Console.WriteLine("This feature is under development.");
5  }
```

When choosing a diagnostic code to pass in the ExperimentalAttribute, choose something that starts with letters and ends in numbers. If you make the prefix unique, then you won't have to worry about stepping on other diagnostic codes. Here we use "EXP" as our prefix, but any unique name can be chosen.

Note: When you try to build the method with the experimental method and you are trying to call it in your code, you may get a compilation error. To get it to build properly, you will need to change the severity of the error to warning.

C# 12.0 continues to evolve the language with a focus on safety, simplicity, and expressiveness. These features each address specific needs in modern software development, from performance improvements with `ref readonly` parameters to simplifications in code verbosity with primary constructors and inline arrays. By leveraging these features, developers can write more efficient, clear, and maintainable C# code.

Chapter 11: New Features in C# 13.0

C# 13.0 introduces several new features and enhancements designed to improve the language's functionality and usability. Here are the key features:

C# 13 Setup

As of this book writing, first you will need to install the .NET 9 preview[1].

In order to use the new features in C# 13, you need to set the language in the project file to **preview**. You will also need to set **EnablePreviewFeatures** to true.

```
1  <PropertyGroup>
2    <OutputType>Exe</OutputType>
3    <TargetFramework>net9.0</TargetFramework>
4    <LangVersion>preview</LangVersion>
5    <EnablePreviewFeatures>true</EnablePreviewFeatures>
6    <RootNamespace>Evolution_11_net9</RootNamespace>
7    <ImplicitUsings>enable</ImplicitUsings>
8    <Nullable>enable</Nullable>
9  </PropertyGroup>
```

You also have to go into the Visual Studio Menu and set Tools—>Options—>Environment—>Preview Features and check **Use Preview of the .NET SDK (requires restart)**

---

[1] https://dotnet.microsoft.com/en-us/download/dotnet/9.0

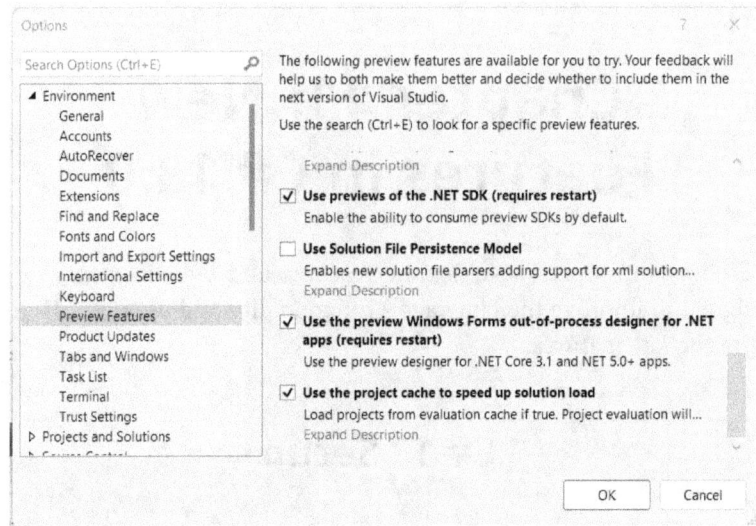

Figure 1. Preview Setup

Params Collections:

- The `params` modifier is now extended beyond arrays to support any recognized collection type. This includes `System.Span<T>`, `System.ReadOnlySpan<T>`, and types implementing `IEnumerable<T>` with an `Add` method. This allows for more flexible method signatures and parameter passing. See the example below:

```
public class Example
{
    public void AddItems(params List<int> items)
    {
        foreach (var item in items)
        {
            Console.WriteLine(item);
        }
    }
}
```

To call the method use the following code:

```
new Example().AddItems(1,2,3);
```

New Lock Type :

- A new synchronization type, System.Threading.Lock, has been introduced to provide better thread synchronization. The Lock.EnterScope() method allows entering an exclusive scope, and the ref struct returned supports the Dispose() pattern to exit the scope. This offers a more robust and intuitive API for managing thread synchronization.

The new lock type introduced in C# 13.0, System.Threading.Lock, provides a more modern and efficient way to handle thread synchronization. This type supports better thread synchronization through its API and uses a ref struct returned from the EnterScope method to manage the lock scope.

Here's an example demonstrating how to use the new Lock type:

Chapter 11: New Features in C# 13.0

```csharp
using System;
using System.Threading;

public class LockExample
{
    private Lock _lock = new Lock();

    public void CriticalSection()
    {
        // Using the new Lock type to enter
        // an exclusive scope
        using (_lock.EnterScope())
        {
            // Critical section code here
            Console.WriteLine(
                "Entering critical section.");
            Thread.Sleep(1000);  // Simulate work
            Console.WriteLine(
                "Exiting critical section.");
        }
    }
}

class Program
{
    static void Main()
    {
        var example = new LockExample();

        // Create multiple threads to test the lock
        var threads = new Thread[3];
        for (int i = 0; i < threads.Length; i++)
        {
            threads[i] = new Thread(
                    example.CriticalSection);
```

```
            threads[i].Start();
        }

        // Wait for all threads to complete
        foreach (var thread in threads)
        {
            thread.Join();
        }

        Console.WriteLine("All threads completed.");
    }
}
```

Explanation

1. **Lock Initialization**: An instance of the Lock class is created (private Lock _lock = new Lock();).
2. **Entering the Lock Scope**: The EnterScope method of the Lock instance is called within a using statement to enter an exclusive scope. This ensures that the lock is properly released when the scope is exited.
3. **Critical Section**: Inside the using block, the critical section code is placed. This code will be executed by only one thread at a time, ensuring thread safety.
4. **Simulating Work**: A Thread.Sleep(1000) call is used to simulate some work being done within the critical section.
5. **Multi-threading Test**: Multiple threads are created and started to test the lock. Each thread runs the CriticalSection method, and they will be synchronized by the Lock instance.
6. **Waiting for Threads**: The Main method waits for all threads to complete using thread.Join().

This example demonstrates the basic usage of the new Lock type for thread synchronization in C# 13.0, making it easier to write safe and efficient multi-threaded code.

New Escape Sequence:

- The escape sequence \e has been added to represent the ESCAPE character (Unicode U+001B). This provides a simpler and more readable way to include the escape character in strings compared to using \u001b or \x1b.

For example, The code below shows the better readability in using the new escape.

```
using System;

class Program
{
    static void Main()
    {
        // Using the new \e escape sequence to
        // represent the ESCAPE character
        string escapeSequence =
            "\e[31mThis text is red!\e[0m";

        // Displaying the string with the escape
        // sequence
        Console.WriteLine(escapeSequence);

        // Alternative methods for the same escape
        // character
        string escapeSequenceAlt1 =
            "\u001b[31mThis text is red!\u001b[0m";
        string escapeSequenceAlt2 =
            "\x1b[31mThis text is red!\x1b[0m";
```

```
22
23            // Displaying the alternative strings with
24            // escape sequences
25            Console.WriteLine(escapeSequenceAlt1);
26            Console.WriteLine(escapeSequenceAlt2);
27        }
28    }
```

Explanation

1. **New Escape Sequence**: The string `"\e[31mThis text is red!\e[0m"` uses the new `\e` escape sequence to represent the ESCAPE character. This is often used in terminal control sequences to change text color.
2. **Displaying the String**: The `Console.WriteLine` method is used to print the string. If the terminal or console supports ANSI escape codes, the text "This text is red!" will be displayed in red.
3. **Alternative Methods**: The same ESCAPE character can be represented using `"\u001b"` or `"\x1b"`. These methods are included for comparison.

This example shows how the new `\e` escape sequence makes it easier and more readable to include the ESCAPE character in strings, improving code clarity and maintainability.

Method Group Natural Type Improvements:

The method group natural type improvements in C# 13.0 aim to optimize the compiler's process for resolving method overloads involving method groups. This enhancement allows the compiler to more accurately and efficiently determine the natural type of a method group by pruning non-applicable candidate methods earlier in the resolution process.

Here's an example to demonstrate how these improvements work:

Example Scenario

Consider a scenario where we have overloaded methods with different parameter types, and we use method groups to select the appropriate overload.

Original Code (C# 12.0 and earlier)

```
using System;

public class Example
{
    public void PrintMessage(string message)
    {
        Console.WriteLine($"String: {message}");
    }

    public void PrintMessage(int number)
    {
        Console.WriteLine($"Integer: {number}");
    }

    public void Execute(Action<string> action)
    {
        action("Hello from string");
    }

    public void Execute(Action<int> action)
    {
```

```
            action(42);
        }
    }

    class Program
    {
        static void Main()
        {
            var example = new Example();

            // Using method group to select the
            // appropriate overload
            example.Execute(example.PrintMessage);
                // This
                // will cause ambiguity in older versions
        }
    }
```

In versions prior to C# 13.0, the compiler might have difficulty resolving which PrintMessage method to use, potentially resulting in an ambiguity error.

Improved Code with C# 13.0

With the method group natural type improvements in C# 13.0, the compiler more effectively determines the applicable method group, reducing ambiguity.

Chapter 11: New Features in C# 13.0

```csharp
using System;

public class Example
{
    public void PrintMessage(string message)
    {
        Console.WriteLine($"String: {message}");
    }

    public void PrintMessage(int number)
    {
        Console.WriteLine($"Integer: {number}");
    }

    public void Execute(Action<string> action)
    {
        action("Hello from string");
    }

    public void Execute(Action<int> action)
    {
        action(42);
    }
}

class Program
{
    static void Main()
    {
        var example = new Example();

        // Using method group to select the
        // appropriate overload
        example.Execute(
            (Action<string>)example.PrintMessage);
```

```
36                    // Explicitly casting to
37                    // resolve ambiguity
38            example.Execute(
39                (Action<int>)example.PrintMessage);
40                    // Explicitly casting
41                    // to resolve ambiguity
42        }
43    }
```

Explanation

1. **Method Group**: The `example.Execute(example.PrintMessage)` line uses a method group, which refers to all overloads of `PrintMessage`.
2. **Explicit Casting**: By explicitly casting the method group to `Action<string>` or `Action<int>`, we inform the compiler of the exact overload to use. In C# 13.0, the compiler's improved algorithm helps resolve such cases more naturally and efficiently, though explicit casting can still be used to eliminate any remaining ambiguity.

Benefits of the Improvement

- **Efficiency**: The compiler prunes the set of candidate methods earlier in the process, improving performance.
- **Accuracy**: By eliminating non-applicable methods earlier, the compiler more accurately determines the correct method overload.
- **Reduced Ambiguity**: The natural type determination process is more reliable, reducing the likelihood of ambiguity errors in complex method group scenarios.

These improvements make it easier for developers to work with method groups and overloaded methods, enhancing both performance and code clarity.

Implicit Indexer Access in Object Initializers:

- The ^ operator, which allows indexing from the end of a collection, can now be used in object initializers. This improvement makes it easier to initialize collections and arrays in a more intuitive way. For example, you can now initialize an array in an object initializer with reversed indexing⊠28†source⊠.

The ^ operator in C# is known as the index-from-end operator. It allows you to access elements in a collection from the end, providing a convenient and readable way to reference elements relative to the end of an array, string, or other collection types. Here are some examples to illustrate how it is used:

Example 1: Accessing Elements from the End of an Array

```csharp
using System;

class Program
{
    static void Main()
    {
        int[] numbers = { 1, 2, 3, 4, 5 };

        // Accessing elements from the end using
        // the ^ operator
        Console.WriteLine(numbers[^1]); // Output: 5
                                        // (last element)
        Console.WriteLine(numbers[^2]); // Output: 4
                            // (second to last element)
    }
}
```

In this example:

- `numbers[^1]` accesses the last element of the array.
- `numbers[^2]` accesses the second to last element.

Example 2: Slicing Arrays with the ^ Operator

The ^ operator can also be combined with ranges to create slices of arrays:

Chapter 11: New Features in C# 13.0

```csharp
using System;

class Program
{
    static void Main()
    {
        int[] numbers = { 1, 2, 3, 4, 5 };

        // Creating slices using ranges and
        // the ^ operator
        int[] lastTwo = numbers[^2..];   // Last two
                                         // elements: { 4, 5 }
        int[] middleThree = numbers[1..^1]; // Middle
                                            // three
                                            // elements:
                                            // { 2, 3, 4 }

        Console.WriteLine(
            string.Join(", ", lastTwo));
                                // Output: 4, 5
        Console.WriteLine(
            string.Join(", ", middleThree));
                                // Output: 2, 3, 4
    }
}
```

In this example:

- numbers[^2..] creates a slice starting from the second to last element to the end of the array.
- numbers[1..^1] creates a slice from the second element to the second to last element.

Example 3: Using the ^ Operator with Strings

The ^ operator can be used with strings to access characters from the end:

```
using System;

class Program
{
    static void Main()
    {
        string text = "Hello, World!";

        // Accessing characters from the end using
        // the ^ operator
        Console.WriteLine(text[^1]); // Output: !
        Console.WriteLine(text[^2]); // Output: d
    }
}
```

In this example:

- text[^1] accesses the last character of the string.
- text[^2] accesses the second to last character.

Example 4: Using the ^ Operator in Object Initializers

Now that we understand how the ^ operator is used in array manipulation, let's see how the ^ operator can be used in object initializers to access and set elements from the end of a buffer:

Chapter 11: New Features in C# 13.0

```csharp
using System;

public class TimerRemaining
{
    public int[] buffer;

    public TimerRemaining(int size)
    {
        buffer = new int[size];
    }
}

class Program
{
    static void Main()
    {
        var countdown = new TimerRemaining(10)
        {
            buffer =
            {
                [^1] = 0,
                [^2] = 1,
                [^3] = 2,
                [^4] = 3,
                [^5] = 4,
                [^6] = 5,
                [^7] = 6,
                [^8] = 7,
                [^9] = 8,
                [^10] = 9
            }
        };

        foreach (var item in countdown.buffer)
        {
```

```
36              Console.WriteLine(item);
37          }
38      }
39  }
```

The code snippet you provided defines a simple class `TimerRemaining` that encapsulates an integer array (`buffer`). The array is intended to represent a timer's countdown values.

Here's a detailed breakdown of the components and functionality of your code:

1. **Class Definition**:

    - **TimerRemaining**: This class has a single public field, `buffer`, which is an array of integers. The constructor of the class accepts an integer `size` which initializes the `buffer` array to that size.

2. **Class Instance Creation and Initialization**:

    - **Main Method**: Inside the `Main` method of the `Program` class, an instance of `TimerRemaining` is created with the buffer size of 10.
    - **Object Initializer**: Immediately after instantiation, the buffer array is initialized using an object initializer that utilizes index-from-end (^) operators. This syntax [^1] = 0, [^2] = 1, and so on, sets the array's elements in reverse order. The ^1 index represents the last element of the array, ^2 the second to last, and so forth.

3. **Array Initialization Explained**:

    - The indices [^1], [^2], ... [^10] refer to the positions starting from the end of the array. This approach essentially fills the array with values from 0 to 9 but in reverse order, where 0 is at the last position and 9 at the first.

4. **Output Display**:

    - **Loop**: A `foreach` loop iterates over the `buffer` array, printing each element to the console. Due to the reverse ordering in the initialization step, the output will display numbers from 9 to 0, effectively creating a countdown effect.

This setup is particularly useful when you need to initialize an array in a non-standard order directly within an object initializer. The usage of the index-from-end operator (^) provides a concise way to address elements in reverse without calculating specific index positions, enhancing code readability and maintainability.

The ^ operator provides a concise and intuitive way to work with elements from the end of collections in C#, enhancing readability and reducing the potential for errors in index calculations. Its integration with array slicing and object initializers further extends its usefulness in various scenarios.

These features are part of the ongoing efforts to make C# a more powerful and user-friendly language, enhancing both performance and developer experience. You can try these features using the latest .NET 9 Preview SDK and Visual Studio 2022 Preview.

For more details, you can refer to the official documentation on Microsoft Learn[2] and the GitHub documentation[3].

---

[2] https://learn.microsoft.com/en-us/dotnet/csharp/whats-new/csharp-13
[3] https://github.com/dotnet/docs/blob/main/docs/csharp/whats-new/csharp-13.md

Appendix: Resources for Exploring the Evolution of C#

1. Accessing the Source Code on GitHub

The evolution of C# has been a fascinating journey, marked by continuous improvements and innovative features. For those who want to delve deeper into the specifics of each version, exploring the source code can be incredibly valuable. The complete source code that demonstrates the evolution of C# from version 7.0 to 13.0 is available on GitHub. Here's how you can access it:

GitHub Repository:

- **URL:** CSharp-Evolution Repository[4]
- **Repository Name:** CSharp-Evolution
- **Owner:** microgold

Steps to Access:

1. Open your web browser and navigate to https://github.com/microgold/CSharp-Evolution.
2. On the repository page, you can browse the different folders and files corresponding to each version of C#.
3. Each folder contains examples and documentation that highlight the new features introduced in that particular version.

Cloning the Repository: If you prefer to explore the code on your local machine, you can clone the repository using Git:

```
git clone https://github.com/microgold/CSharp-Evolution.g\
it
```

Once cloned, you can navigate through the code using your favorite code editor or IDE.

---

[4]https://github.com/microgold/CSharp-Evolution

2. Reading Official Facts on the Microsoft Site

For authoritative information and official documentation, the Microsoft site is an excellent resource. Here are some key places where you can find detailed facts about C# and its evolution:

Microsoft Docs:

- **C# Documentation Overview:** docs.microsoft.com/dotnet/csharp[5]
- This comprehensive resource provides in-depth documentation on C# language features, syntax, and best practices.

Specific Versions:

- **C# 7.x Documentation:** docs.microsoft.com/dotnet/csharp/whats-new/csharp-7[6]
- **C# 8.0 Documentation:** docs.microsoft.com/dotnet/csharp/whats-new/csharp-8[7]
- **C# 9.0 Documentation:** docs.microsoft.com/dotnet/csharp/whats-new/csharp-9[8]
- **C# 10.0 Documentation:** docs.microsoft.com/dotnet/csharp/whats-new/csharp-10[9]
- **C# 11.0 Documentation:** docs.microsoft.com/dotnet/csharp/whats-new/csharp-11[10]
- **C# 12.0 Documentation:** docs.microsoft.com/dotnet/csharp/whats-new/csharp-12[11]

Blogs and Announcements:

- **.NET Blog:** devblogs.microsoft.com/dotnet[12]

---

[5] https://docs.microsoft.com/dotnet/csharp
[6] https://docs.microsoft.com/dotnet/csharp/whats-new/csharp-7
[7] https://docs.microsoft.com/dotnet/csharp/whats-new/csharp-8
[8] https://docs.microsoft.com/dotnet/csharp/whats-new/csharp-9
[9] https://docs.microsoft.com/dotnet/csharp/whats-new/csharp-10
[10] https://docs.microsoft.com/dotnet/csharp/whats-new/csharp-11
[11] https://docs.microsoft.com/dotnet/csharp/whats-new/csharp-12
[12] https://devblogs.microsoft.com/dotnet

- This blog features announcements, detailed explanations of new features, and discussions on the future directions of C# and .NET.

Community and Discussion:

- **C# Language Design Discussions:** github.com/dotnet/csharplang[13]
- This repository contains discussions, proposals, and design notes from the C# language design team.

3. Summary and Additional Resources

By leveraging these resources, you can gain a thorough understanding of how C# has evolved over the years. The GitHub repository provides practical examples and hands-on experience, while the Microsoft documentation and blogs offer detailed explanations and the latest updates.

Additional Resources:

- **C# GitHub Discussions:** Engage with the community and contribute to discussions about the language.
- **Microsoft Learn:** Interactive tutorials and learning paths for mastering C# and .NET.

These resources will not only help you understand the historical context and technical details of each version but also keep you updated with the latest advancements and best practices in C# development.

---

[13] https://github.com/dotnet/csharplang

www.ingramcontent.com/pod-product-compliance
Lightning Source LLC
Chambersburg PA
CBHW071918210526
45479CB00002B/460